🔊 AUDIO ACCESS INCLUDED
Recorded Performances and Accompaniments Online

LEVEL 1

Singing Kids' Songbook

DANA LENTINI

To access companion recorded performances and
piano accompaniments online, visit:
www.halleonard.com/mylibrary
Enter Code
6247-5964-7398-3950

ISBN 978-1-70514-854-9

Copyright © 2022 by HAL LEONARD LLC
International Copyright Secured All Rights Reserved

No part of this publication may be reproduced in any form or by
any means without the prior written permission of the Publisher.

Visit Hal Leonard Online at
www.halleonard.com

World headquarters, contact:
Hal Leonard
7777 West Bluemound Road
Milwaukee, WI 53213
Email: info@halleonard.com

In Europe, contact:
Hal Leonard Europe Limited
1 Red Place
London, W1K 6PL
Email: info@halleonardeurope.com

In Australia, contact:
Hal Leonard Australia Pty. Ltd.
4 Lentara Court
Cheltenham, Victoria, 3192 Australia
Email: info@halleonard.com.au

Singing Kids' Songbook Series

LEVEL 1
About This Book

This progressive songbook series is designed to guide and create knowledgeable, developing singers as they seek awareness and study the art of singing. Each of the books focuses on different ages and stages of development.

Level 1 is designed to be the discovery point for early and beginning singers. Young singers will dig deeper into foundational skills required for nurturing and enhancing the coordination of mind, body, musicality, and heart in singing. Techniques are introduced through fun and engaging exercises to assist with refinement and practice.

In these pages you will find a scaffolding of songs and strategies, eliminating the potential challenges of repertoire selection and lesson planning for both singer and teacher. Original, traditional, and popular songs are included to introduce a wide variety of styles. The carefully devised objectives lead naturally to capable outcomes for kids, allowing for confidence building and mastery of skills.

Basic singing and musical skills including expression, articulation, diction, form, pitch matching, pitch motion, vocal exploration (registration), rhythm, and performance etiquette are introduced in progressive order. A "Singer's Choice" activity page at the end of the book guides young singers working on additional selections.

This book would not be complete without a thank you to Brendan Fox and Rick Walters at Hal Leonard for helping me create this songbook and their work in bringing it to life. A big thanks to our young singers for adding their voices to this project, and to Kristina Driskill, who is a constant source of light on my teaching journey. And thank YOU for adding this songbook to your library.

–Dana Lentini

Table of Contents

4	Solfege Chart
5	#1 **I Am a Robot**[2]
11	#2 **BINGO**[1]
16	#3 **Twinkle, Twinkle, Little Star**[2]
23	#4 **Umbrellas**[4]
27	#5 **Lavender's Blue**[7]
32	#6 **I Like to Sing My ABCs**[8]
38	#7 **Do-Re-Mi**[1]
44	#8 **Growl and Howl**[3]
52	#9 **My Country, 'Tis of Thee**[7]
56	#10 **Sleep Gently, Tiny Child**[2]
62	#11 **Come On Get Happy**[5]
70	#12 **Tell Me Your Story**[6]
78	#13 **Cleaning!**[2]
84	#14 **Catch a Falling Star**[7]
91	#15 **A Step in the Right Direction**[6]
99	Singer's Choice Activity
101	Song Lyrics
107	Certificate

Singers on recordings: [1] Nora Burzlaff (age 7), [2] Penny Burzlaff (age 6), [3] Connor Cosmo Buxton (age 13), [4] Julianna A. Buxton (age 10), [5] Beatrice Hart (age 9), [6] Karenna Klein (age 13), [7] Annalise Nordstrom (age 9), [8] Charlotte Piedlow (age 7)
Pianist: Brendan Fox

Solfege Chart

Kodály Hand Signs

Do'

Ti

La

Sol

Fa

Mi

Re

Do

SONG #1
I Am a Robot

PREPARATION

Listen to this song while moving to the beat.
What happens to the robot at the end of the song?

_____

When you move to the beat how does your movement change at the end?

_____

ACTIVITY
Draw a picture of your robot.

MUSICAL CONCEPT: Pitch Matching

Echo your teacher as they sing each small phrase to you. Try singing it back on the same pitch as your teacher. (*Note to teachers: Use whatever starting pitch the singer finds comfortable.*)

DISCOVERY

Musical Treasure Hunt

Look at your vocal score and hunt for symbols. Use your favorite color to circle all the treble clefs 𝄞 you see in your vocal score.

HOW TO PRACTICE

When you practice at home, explore ways to have fun singing and building your skills! Discover other ways your robot can move when you sing this song.

Try out these movements by changing the words.
Circle your favorites and share them with your teacher at your next lesson.

Chop	**Tap**
Sway	**March**
Bend	**Point**
Stretch	**Blink**
Snap	**Smile**
Wave	**Frown**

PERFORMING: Sing from Memory

Once you learn this song, try to memorize all the words and perform it as a solo with the piano accompaniment for your teacher in your lesson.

Singing from memory shows confidence and helps the performer connect with their audience.

A great way to help you memorize your words is to practice singing at home every day!

I AM A ROBOT

Words and Music by
Kymberly Stewart

I AM A ROBOT

Words and Music by
Kymberly Stewart

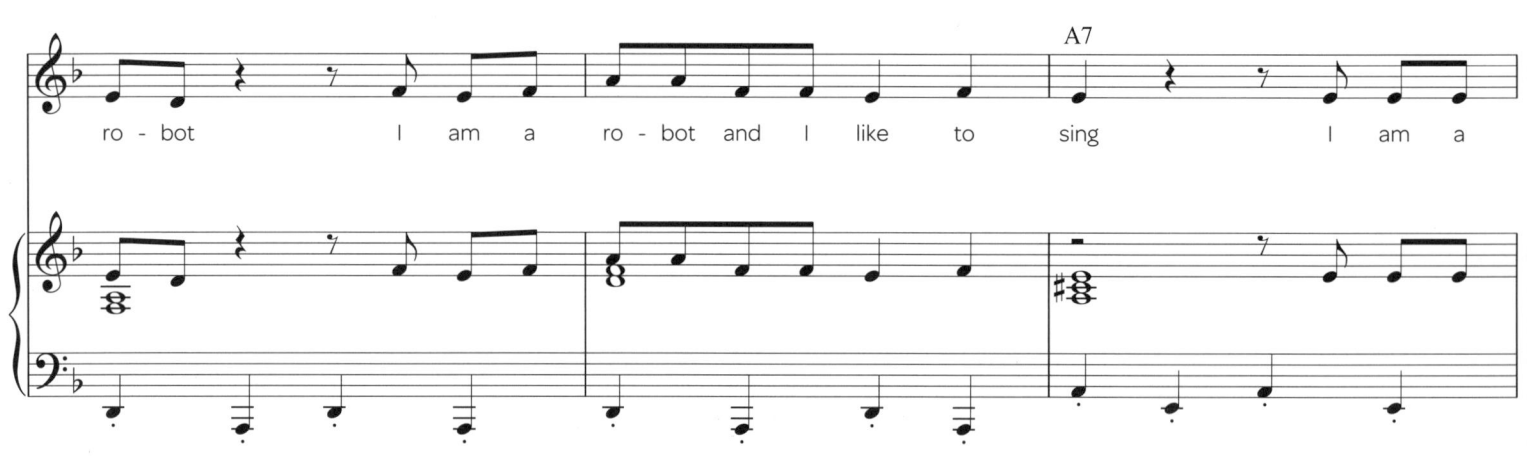
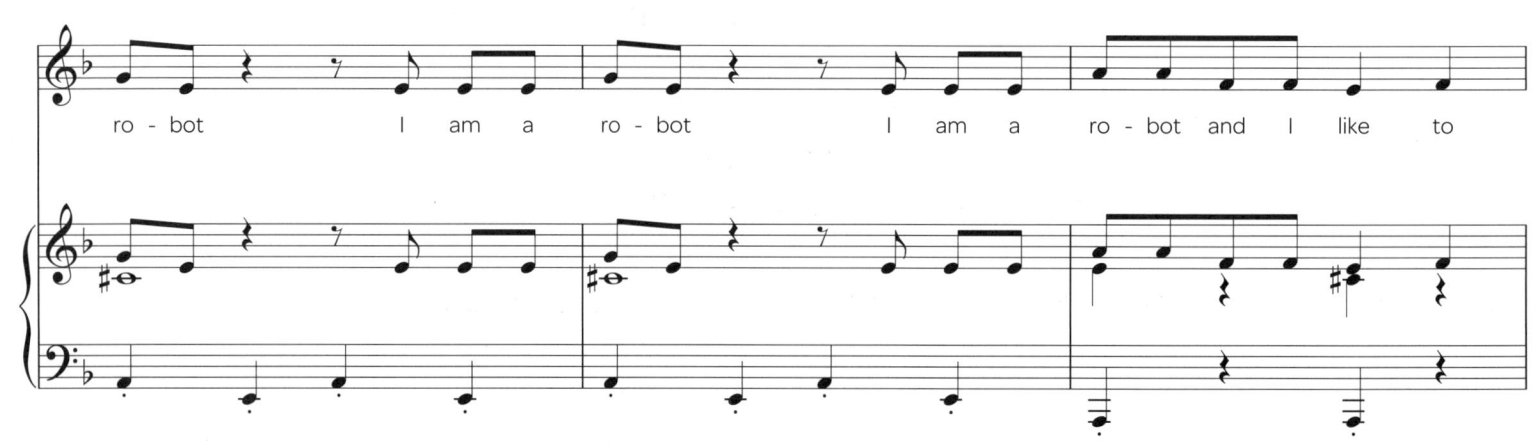

Copyright © 2014 Kymberly Stewart
All Rights Reserved   Used by Permission

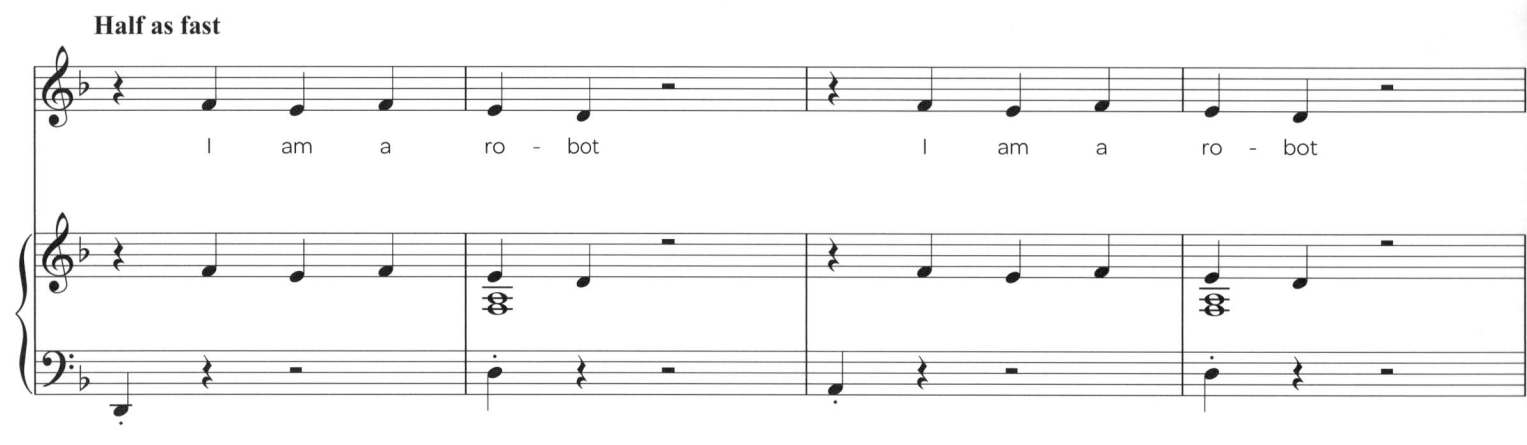

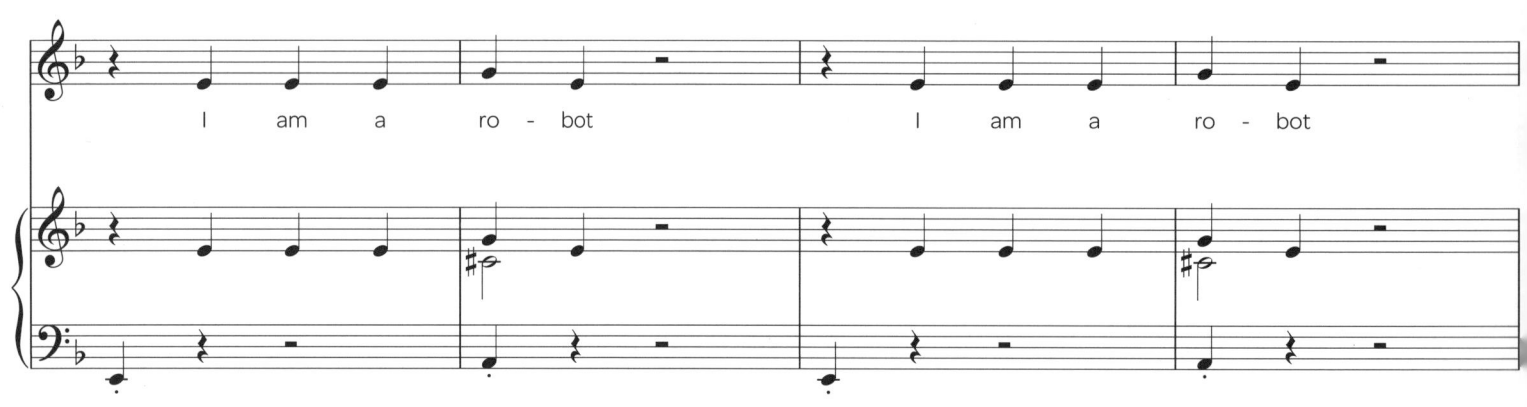
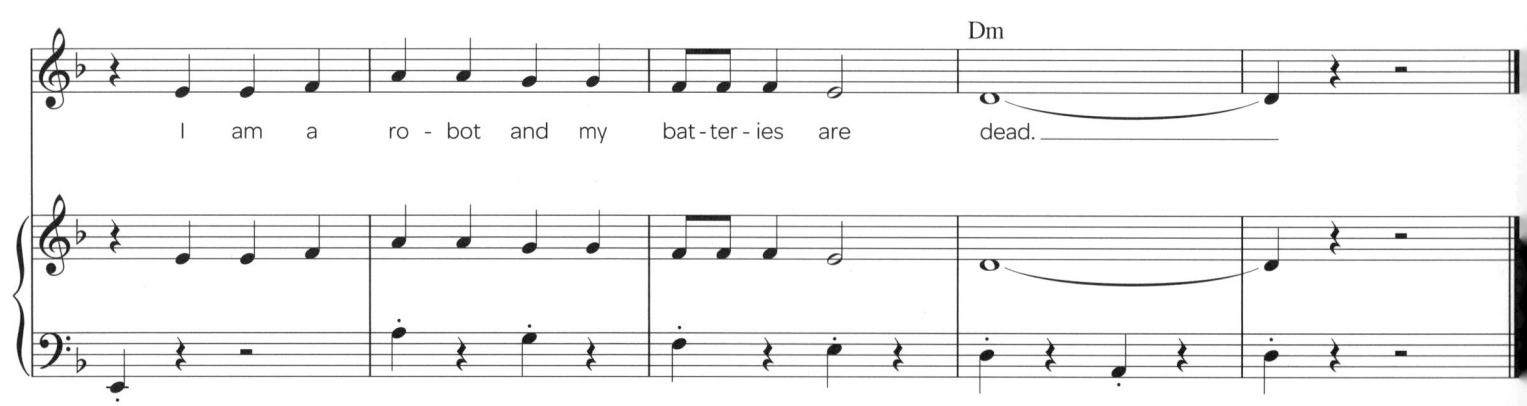

SONG #2
Bingo

PREPARATION

Listen to this song while clapping a steady beat.
What happens to the word BINGO in this song?

_____

ACTIVITY

What kind of dog do you imagine BINGO to be?
Is he a little dog or a big dog?
Does BINGO have short fur, long curly fur, or other?
Draw a picture of your dog BINGO.

MUSICAL CONCEPT: Form In Music

How many times do you repeat the melody in this song? Each time you sing it we call it a verse. After the first verse, the singer drops a letter and claps. Can you count how many claps for each verse?

Verse 1 _____   Verse 2 _____   Verse 3 _____

Verse 4 _____   Verse 3 _____   Verse 6 _____

DISCOVERY

This is called a quarter note: ♩ It gets one count, or beat in music.

These are paired eighth notes: ♫ They get a half count, or beat, each in music.

Clap and count this rhythm with your teacher:

B-I-N-G-O

Musical Treasure Hunt
Hunt in your vocal score and circle the above rhythm wherever you find it.

HOW TO PRACTICE

Connecting to your text and making it your own is one of the best parts of singing. For practice fun at home, change some words to make this song unique to you.

- ☐ Change the word "dog" in the text to another animal that fits the beats.

- ☐ Come up with a new name for your animal with the same amount of letters in *Bingo*.

- ☐ Sing your song replacing "dog" and "Bingo."

PERFORMING: Sing with Expression

Once you memorize all the words and claps, perform this song by expressing the text to tell the story of the farmer and his dog (or another animal that you chose).

When singers express their words with feelings and emotions it is entertaining to the audience.

* Remember: A great way to help you memorize is to sing and listen to your song every day!

BINGO

Traditional

NOTE: Each time a letter of BINGO is deleted in the lyric, clap your hands in place of singing the letter.

BINGO

Traditional

NOTE: Each time a letter of BINGO is deleted in the lyric, clap your hands in place of singing the letter.

SONG #3

Twinkle, Twinkle Little Star

PREPARATION
Carefully listen to the performance recording of this song. How are the verses different from one another?

ACTIVITY
Musicians use solfege syllables and Kodály hand signs to help in learning melodic lines. Practice singing the solfege scale with hand signs. *(See page 4 for solfege chart.)*

Explore singing this song on solfege syllables. Use your favorite colored pencil to write the syllables above the notes in your vocal score.

Try to sing this song using solfege syllables with the hand signs.
Was it easy or hard?

MUSICAL CONCEPT: Articulation
Legato and Staccato are words we use to describe the articulation of the music.

Legato means to sing by connecting the words and notes smoothly together.

Staccato means to detach the words and notes from one another. Staccato notes have dots below each note head that indicate they are to be short and detached.

Listen to the music and discover which verse is legato or staccato. Use an L for legato or an S for staccato and fill in the blanks.

Verse 1 _____   Verse 2 _____   Verse 3 _____

DISCOVERY

Practice this exercise in your vocal warm-up by singing legato and staccato articulation:

Do - Re - Mi - Re - Do   Do - Re - Mi - Re - Do

HOW TO PRACTICE

Practice reading this poem and express words that are meaningful to you:

Starlight, star bright, first star I see tonight:
I wish I may, I wish I might, have this wish I wish tonight.

Highlight the words you feel are important to emphasize.

What are you singing about in the song *Twinkle, Twinkle Little Star*? On another piece of paper, draw a picture of a twinkling star or a picture of yourself singing, or maybe both!
Share it with your teacher in your next lesson.

PERFORMING: Sing to the Audience

Once you master the articulation changes in this song, perform it from memory for your teacher in your lesson.

Singing to your audience can be a little distracting for performers. Find a few spots in the space above and behind your audience and imagine you can see the twinkling star you are singing about.

TWINKLE, TWINKLE LITTLE STAR

Traditional
3rd verse lyrics by Dana Lentini

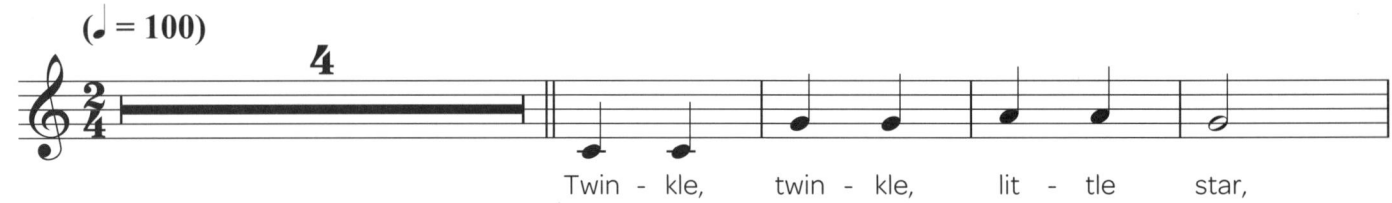

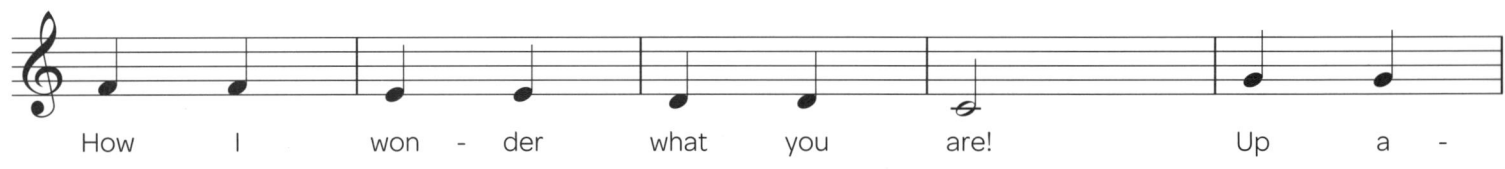

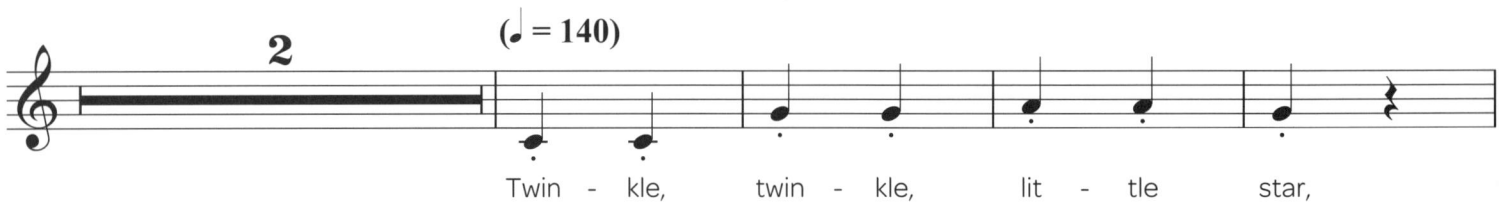

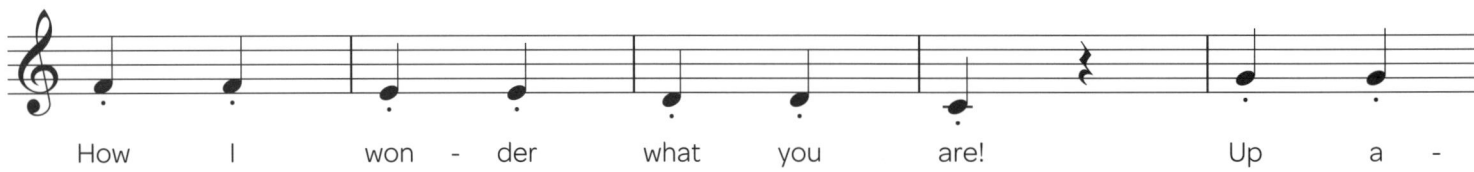

TWINKLE, TWINKLE LITTLE STAR

Traditional
3rd verse lyrics by Dana Lentini

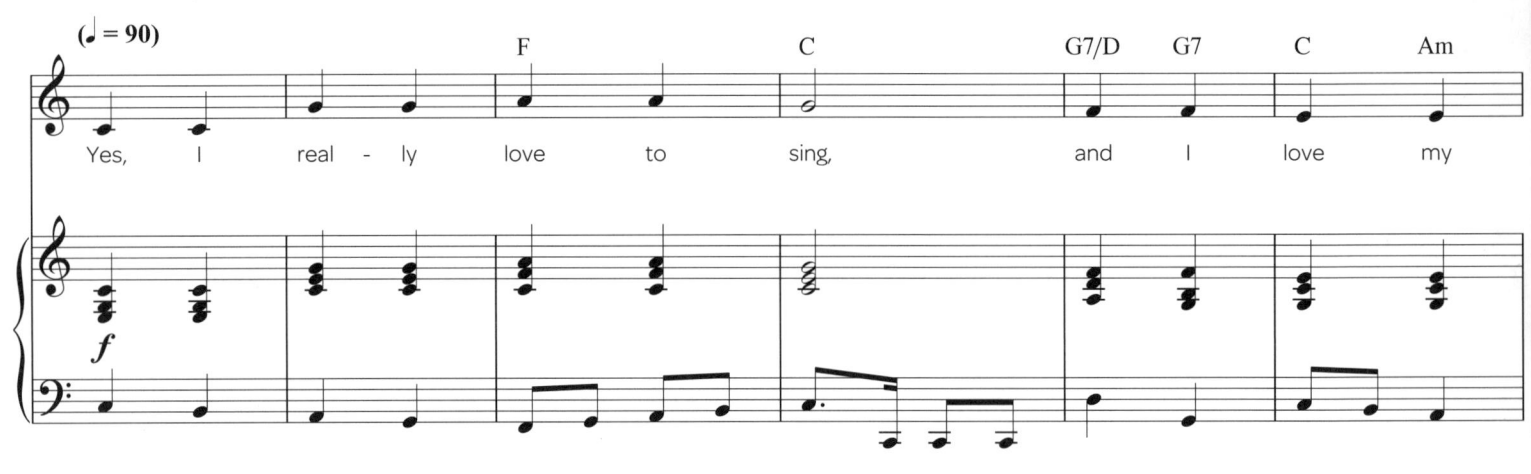
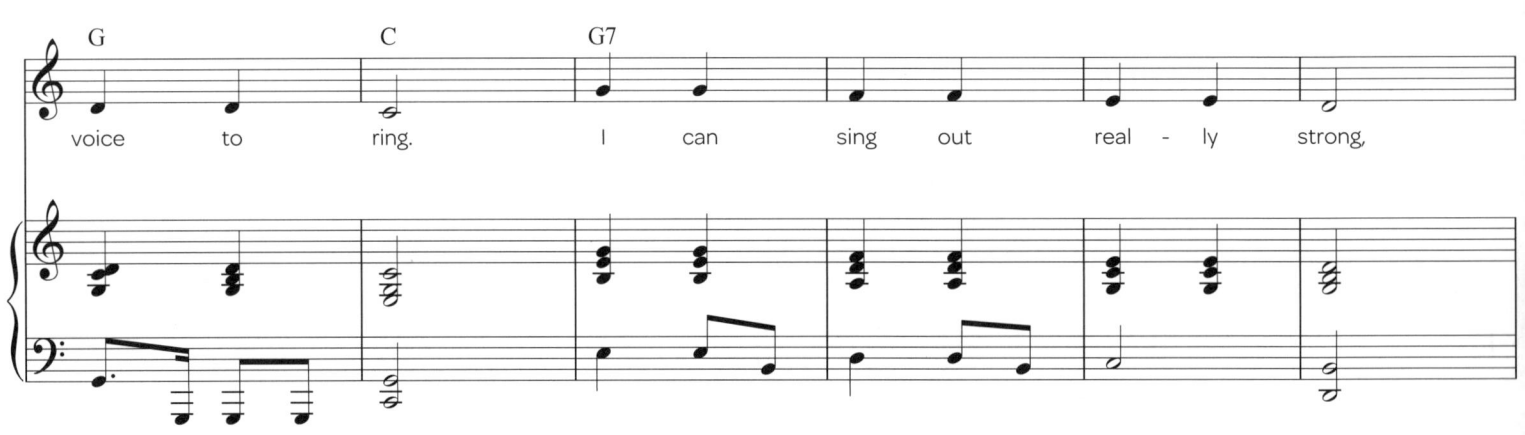
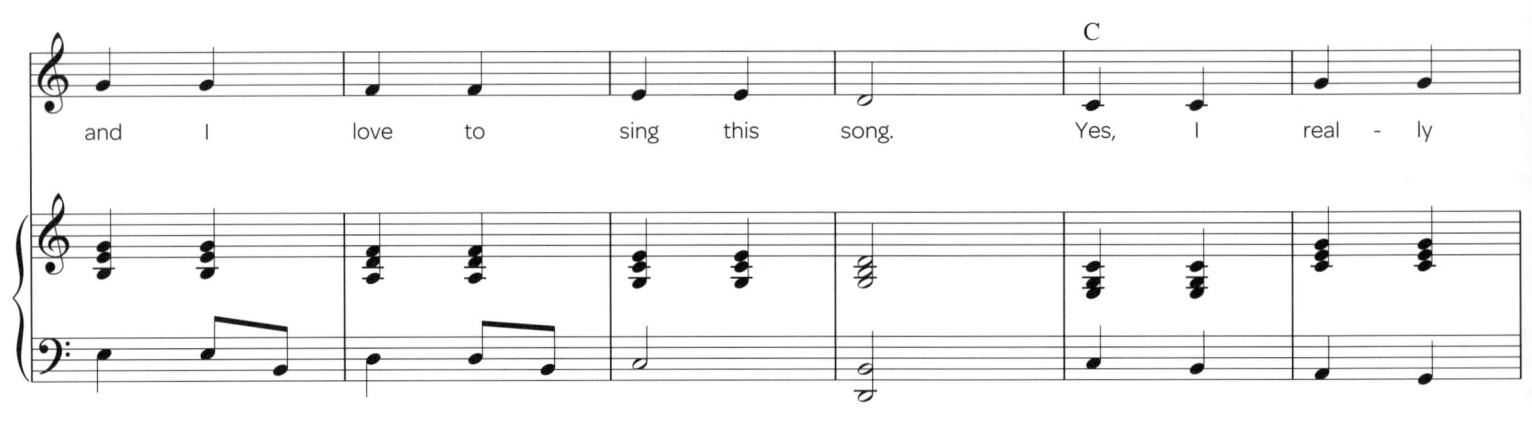

SONG #4
Umbrellas

PREPARATION

A *melody* is a series of notes and rhythms that make a memorable line of music. Listen carefully to the melody in this song. Do you hear ascending (going up) and descending (going down) patterns? Do you hear any repeating notes?

Vocal exploration lines are drawings to represent a flow of sound you can create with your voice. Use the full range of high and low sounds in your voice. In your vocal warm-ups, practice singing these vocal exploration lines. Trace the shape of each line with your voice in a smooth glide. *(Hint: Try to sound like a ghost.)*

Which of these lines is shaped like the melody in this song? Think about where there are ascending patterns, descending patterns, and repeated notes in the song.

ACTIVITY

Echo your teacher singing the melody of this song in small phrases singing on an OO vowel.

SINGING TECHNIQUE:
Vocal Exploration

Follow the shape of the vocal line with a pointer (finger or cursor) and notice when the notes ascend, descend, and repeat.

Circle all of the repeating notes.

DISCOVERY

Musical Treasure Hunt:
Do you remember what this is? ♩
How many quarter notes do you have in this song? _____
(Hint: There are a lot!)

There is one note that is not a quarter note in your melody. Hunt in your vocal score and circle it. What kind of note is it?

Draw what it looks like here. _____   How many beats does it get? _____

HOW TO PRACTICE

What are you singing about in this song? Do you like playing in puddles?
Do you have your own umbrella, raincoat, or rain boots?
Draw a picture of what you look like in the rain:

PERFORMING: Present Yourself

A performance *slate* is an announcement by the performer of your name and the title of the song you are singing. You might also sometimes share who wrote the song. This is an important part of your performance. It helps the audience and the singer prepare for the performance to begin.

My name is _____ .

I will be singing (Title of song) _____.

Practice your slate of this song before you perform it for your teacher. Remember to speak clearly and slowly so listeners can hear and understand you.

UMBRELLAS

Words and Music by
Donna Rhodenizer

Copyright © 2021 Red Castle Publishing
All Rights Reserved   Used by Permission

UMBRELLAS

SONG #5
Lavender's Blue

PREPARATION
Listen to this song while looking at text found on page 102.
Then slowly repeat each line of text after your teacher.

ACTIVITY
Rhymes are words that sound similar.
Many songs are set to poetry and have words that rhyme.
Thinking about the rhyming words helps the singer to memorize their text.
Circle rhyming words you hear in this song.

For practice fun, think of other rhyming words for:

Green_____

Work_____

Corn_____

Blue_____

MUSICAL CONCEPT: Pitch Placement
Write the solfege symbols above the notes in your vocal score. Sing through the melody of this song a cappella, using solfege symbols and Kodály hand signs. (A cappella means to sing unaccompanied)

DISCOVERY

Musical Treasure Hunt:
Signs and symbols in the musical score can tell the performer where to go.
Find these signs in your vocal score and circle them. ||:   :||
These signs tell the performer to go back and repeat something.

27

HOW TO PRACTICE

Speaking and singing with good **diction** means that you are pronouncing words clearly and effectively so the audience can understand what you are singing about.

Warm-up your articulating muscles by repeating these letters:

T-D-T-D-T-D-T-D-T

See if you notice how different the T and D are to pronounce in your mouth.

Speak the text of this song again slowly after you warm up. Practice speaking this every day before your next lesson and see if your teacher can tell the difference in your diction.

Do *you* want to be the king or queen?
Change the words and see if you can make it unique to you.

PERFORMING: Review Performance Skills

Use the rhyming words to help you memorize this song and sing it for an audience so they can understand every word you are singing.

When you are performing, do you remember where to look?
What do you imagine you see out there when singing this song?

LAVENDER'S BLUE

Traditional

Lav - en - der's blue, dil - ly, dil - ly, lav - en - der's green,
Some to make hay, dil - ly, dil - ly, some to cut corn,

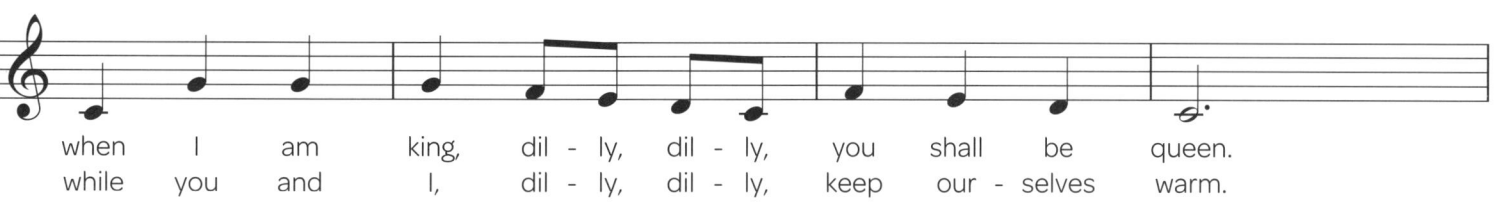

when I am king, dil - ly, dil - ly, you shall be queen.
while you and I, dil - ly, dil - ly, keep our - selves warm.

Call up your men, dil - ly, dil - ly, set them to work.
Lav - en - der's green, dil - ly, dil - ly, lav - en - der's blue,

Some to the plow, dil - ly, dil - ly, some to the cart.
if you love me, dil - ly, dil - ly, I will love you.

LAVENDER'S BLUE

Traditional

SONG #6
I Like to Sing My ABCs

PREPARATION

Listen to this song and see if it sounds like the ABC song you might already know. How is it different?

Listen to the song a second time and move to the beat. Try singing along if you can!

Beat in music is an underlying pulse. It can have an even/steady pulse or the beat can have an uneven/swing pulse. Use your hands to clap or use a percussion instrument to practice feeling the difference.

ACTIVITY

Use your hands to clap or a percussion instrument:

☐ Keep a steady beat with your teacher.

☐ Keep a swing beat with your teacher.

You can have fun creating your own percussion instruments out of household objects!

MUSICAL CONCEPT: Rhythm

Musical Treasure Hunt:

Locate these rhythm patterns in your vocal score:

Use a colored pencil or highlighter to mark in the music where these different patterns occur:

DISCOVERY

With your teacher, practice singing the traditional ABC song (*Twinkle, Twinkle Little Star* melody):

- ☐ Sing it with a steady beat.
- ☐ Sing it with a swing beat.
- ☐ Try changing in the middle of the song from steady to swing beat. Does that feel easy or hard to do?

HOW TO PRACTICE

Work independently to make all your consonants very clear and articulate.
Practice saying this diction poem to warm up your articulator muscles:

Singer's Diction Poem
Tip of the tongue and the teeth
Tip of the tongue and the teeth
Tip of the tongue
And the tip of the tongue
And the tip of the tongue and the teeth

- ☐ Try it while keeping a steady beat.
- ☐ Try it with a swing beat.

Practice this every day before your next lesson!

PERFORMING: Take a Bow!

Learning how to take a bow is an important part of performing.
To take a bow all you have to do is:

1. Bend at your waist
2. Look down at your feet
3. Come back up and smile

This is a nice way to thank your audience for listening.
After you perform this song from memory, practice taking a bow.

If bending at the waist is not comfortable for you, nod your head or gesture with your hand to acknowledge your appreciation.

I LIKE TO SING MY ABC'S

Words and Music by
Kymberly Stewart

I like to sing my A B Cs

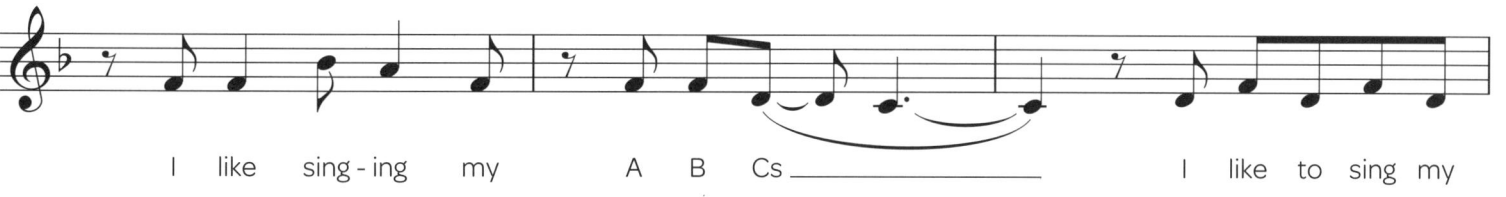
I like sing-ing my A B Cs_____ I like to sing my

A B Cs I like sing-ing my A B Cs_____

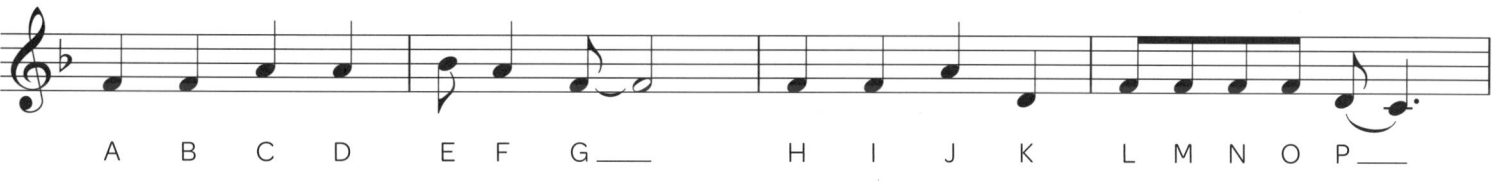
A B C D E F G___ H I J K L M N O P___

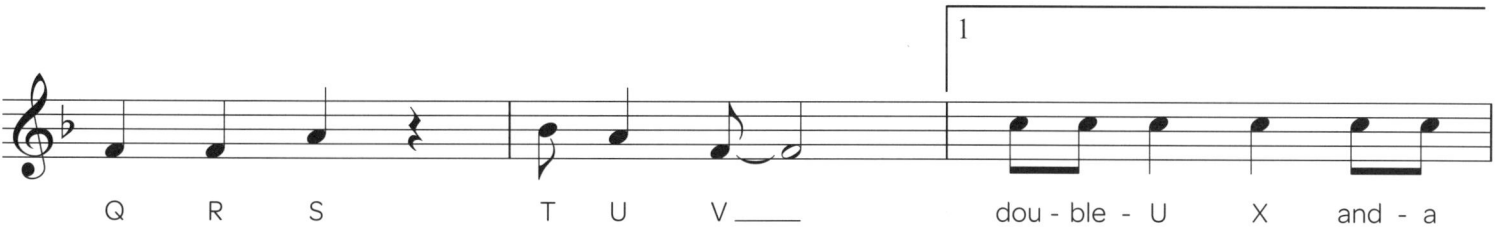
Q R S T U V___ dou-ble-U X and-a

Y and Z___ I sing my dou-ble U X and-a Y and Z

Copyright © 2014 Kymberly Stewart
All Rights Reserved Used by Permission

I LIKE TO SING MY ABC'S

Words and Music by
Kymberly Stewart

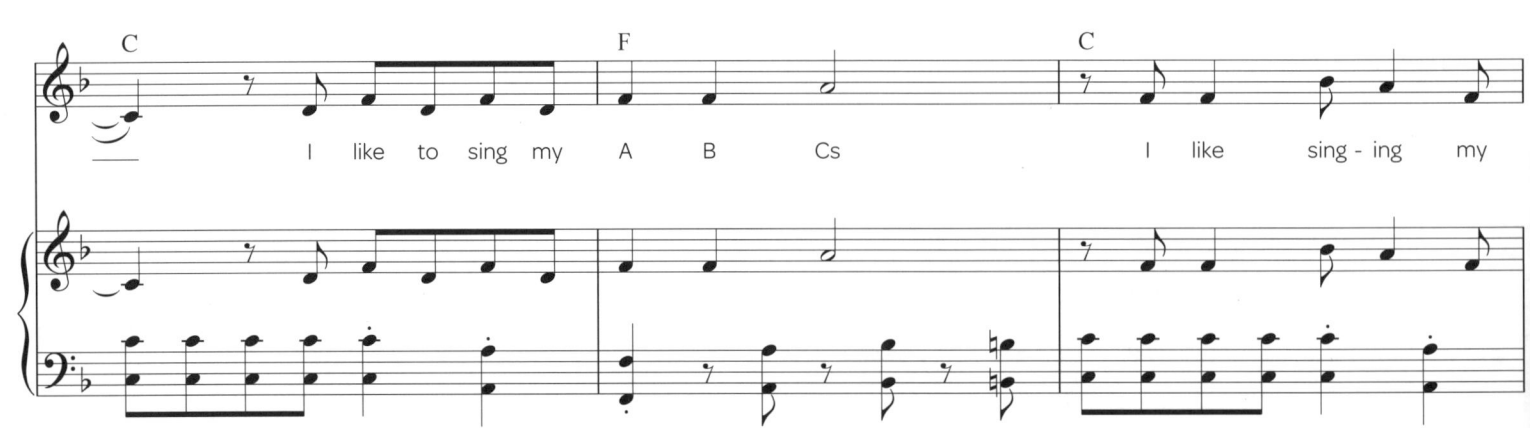

SONG #7
Do-Re-Mi

PREPARATION

Listen to the performance track of this song and see if you can recall the hand signs that accompany each solfege syllable. If you're not sure, look at the Kodály Hand Signs on page 4.

While actively listening to this song a second time, use your hand signs to motion each of the syllables in time with the beat of the music.

ACTIVITY

This song uses descriptive words and symbols that sound like the correct solfege syllable but represent things that you might know. This makes it easy to remember the syllable names.

Match the picture to the correct syllable:

Do　　**So**

Re　　**La**

Me　　**Ti**

Fa　　**Do'**

SINGING TECHNIQUE: Diction

Singing with good diction is important to clearly communicate the story to an audience. To achieve good diction it is good to exercise the muscles that create clear speaking sounds.

Practice speaking this diction poem again. Chant it while keeping a steady beat. Feel the action of your tongue working to get clear letter Ts. After you chant it try singing it on one pitch in different parts of your vocal range.

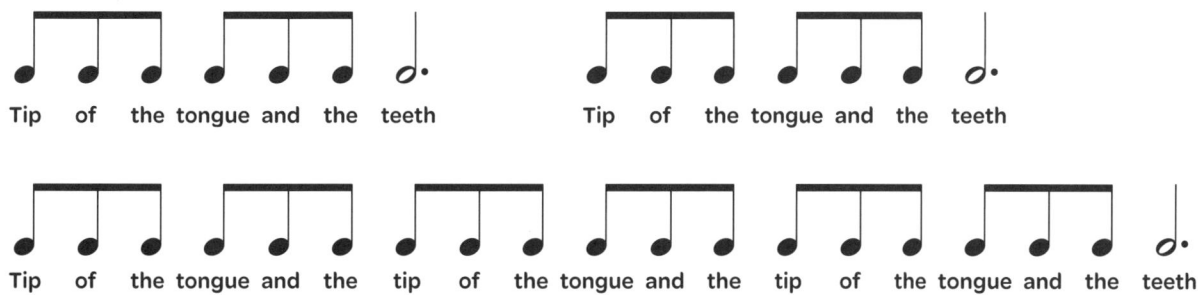

DISCOVERY

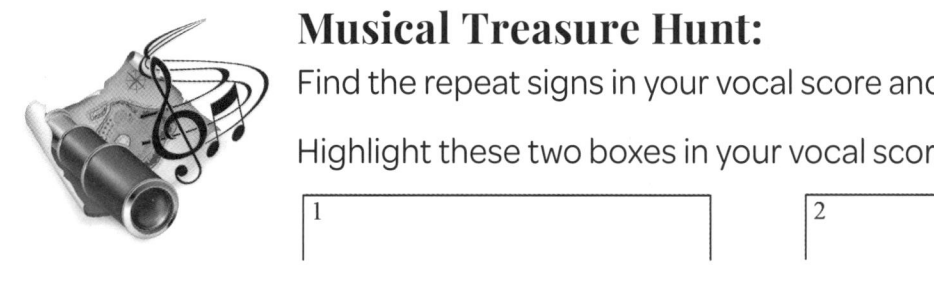

Musical Treasure Hunt:

Find the repeat signs in your vocal score and circle them: ||: :||

Highlight these two boxes in your vocal score:

| 1 | 2 |

These symbols tell us where to go in the music.

When you read to the end of [1] that sign tells you to go back to ||: and sing until [2] ending at the ||

HOW TO PRACTICE

☐ At home, use the diction poem exercises to warm up your articulation muscles every day.

☐ Speak the text for your teacher or a family member and see if they can understand all of your words.

☐ Practice singing this song using hand signs for the solfege syllables or use your own clever gestures to illustrate the meaning of this song.

PERFORMING: Singing Using Gestures

To make this a memorable performance for an audience, depict the story you are singing about. What hand gestures will you use to tell the story?

DO-RE-MI
from The Sound of Music

Lyrics by Oscar Hammerstein II
Music by Richard Rodgers

DO-RE-MI
from *The Sound of Music*

Lyrics by Oscar Hammerstein II
Music by Richard Rodgers

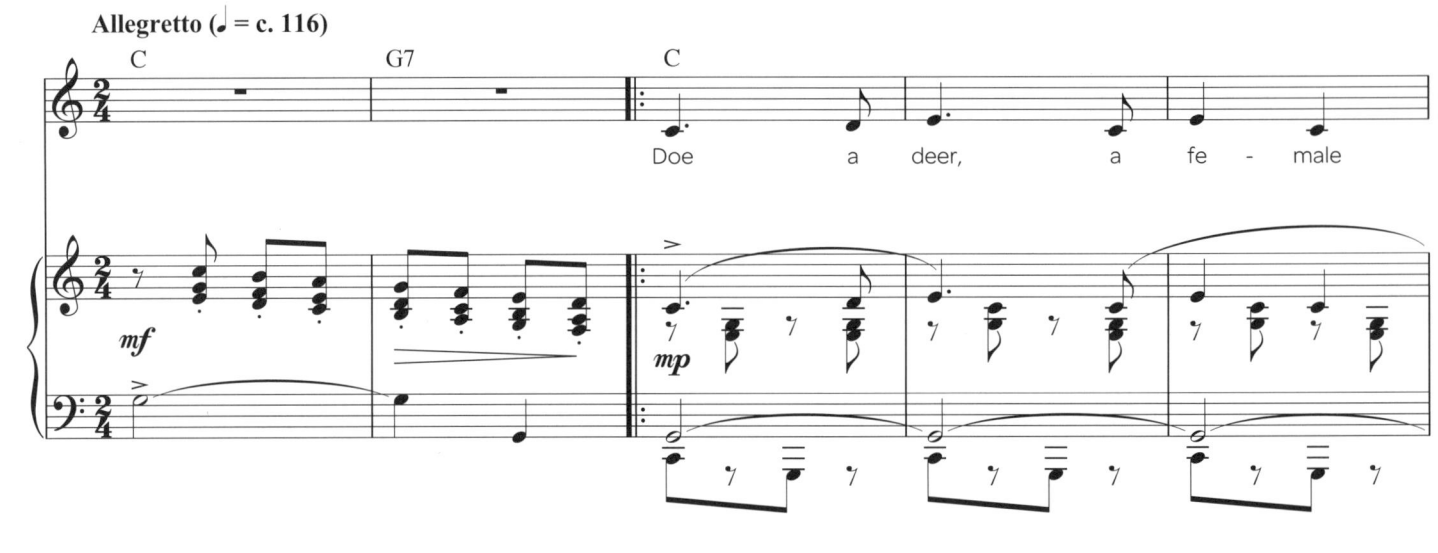
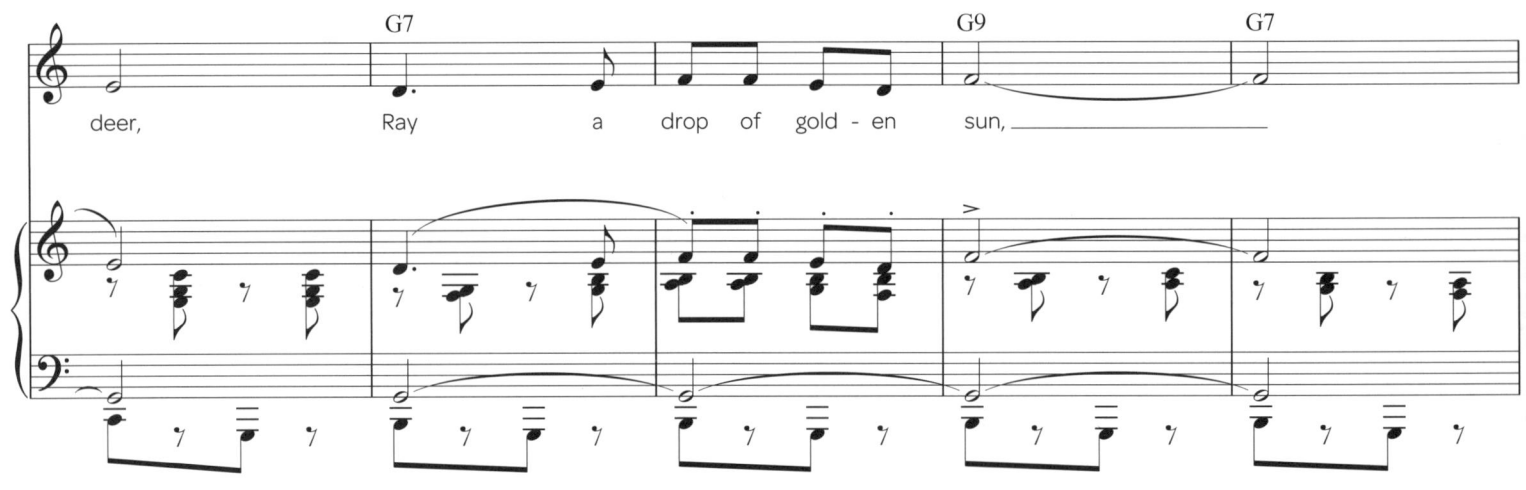
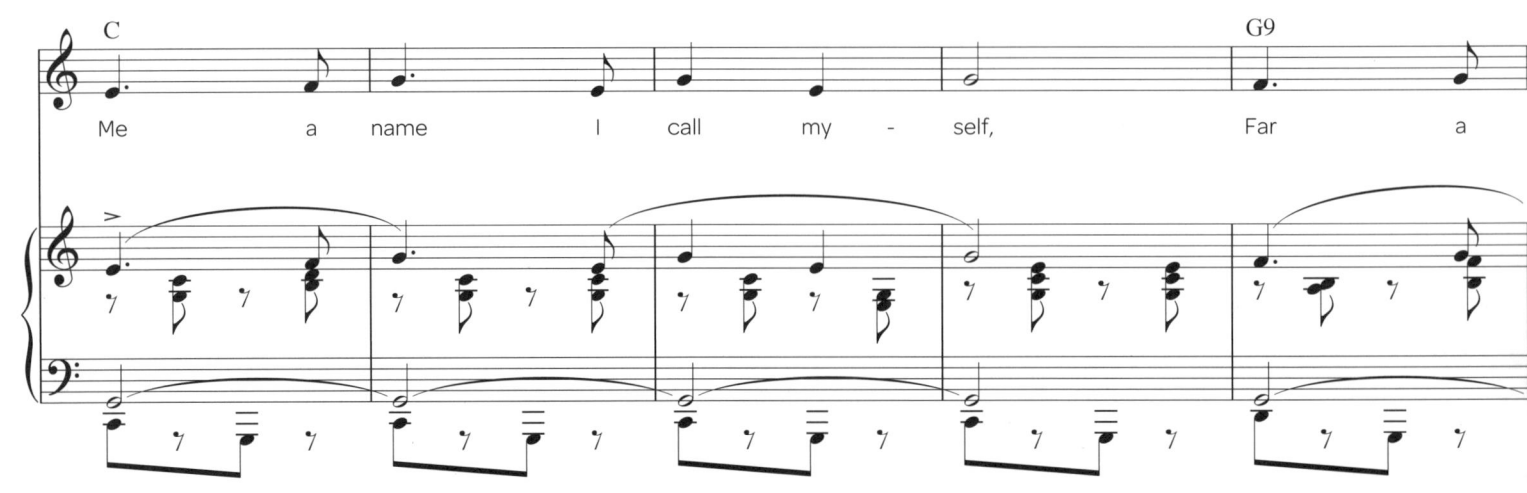

Copyright © 1959 Williamson Music Company c/o Concord Music Publishing
Copyright Renewed
All Rights Reserved   Used by Permission

SONG #8
Growl and Howl

PREPARATION
Listen to this song. How would you describe the feel of the beat? Circle all that apply:

quick   slow   lively   sad   powerful   gentle   happy   fierce

What animal sound is your favorite in this song? _____

ACTIVITY
What is a werewolf?
Draw a picture of what your werewolf looks like:

SINGING TECHNIQUE: Registration
Explore these sounds through the range of your voice using high, low, dark, and light sounds. Try to make sure when you create these sounds that your voice feels free and easy. Don't ever force sounds that feel like they take too much work! Your voice should not feel scratchy or tired after making these sounds.

Grr!	**Woo!**	**Rawr!**
Aa-ooo!	**Meow!**	**Munch!**

Find the above words in your vocal score and circle them.

DISCOVERY

Musical Treasure Hunt:

☐ Have your teacher help you find the tempo marking in your vocal score and circle it.

Fun Fact: **Tempo** means *time* in Italian. The tempo marking tells the performer how fast or slow a piece of music should go.

☐ Circle the word *Pekingese* in your vocal score.

Did you see in your vocal score where it tells you what a Pekingese is? It looks harder to pronounce than it is. Say it like this: Pee-kuh-NEEZ.

☐ Circle the X notes in the score. The X means to make a sound with your voice but not on a musical pitch.

HOW TO PRACTICE

Practice acting out each word below silently and using hand gestures. In your next lesson, see if your teacher can guess which sound you are acting out. Try to make each one different from one another.

Grr!   **Woo!**   **Rawr!**   **Aa-ooo!**   **Meow!**   **Munch!**

PERFORMING: Sing with Exciting Expression!

When you sing this for an audience, act out all the different animal sounds using good facial expressions and gestures with your body and hands.

Tip: Make sure you sing this song using clear and articulate diction so the audience can understand every word, including Pekingese! If you need to work more on making the words clearer, practice speaking the text slowly without singing the music. And use your diction poem exercises to warm-up your articulation muscles.

GROWL AND HOWL

Words by Kendra Preston Leonard
Music by Lisa Neher

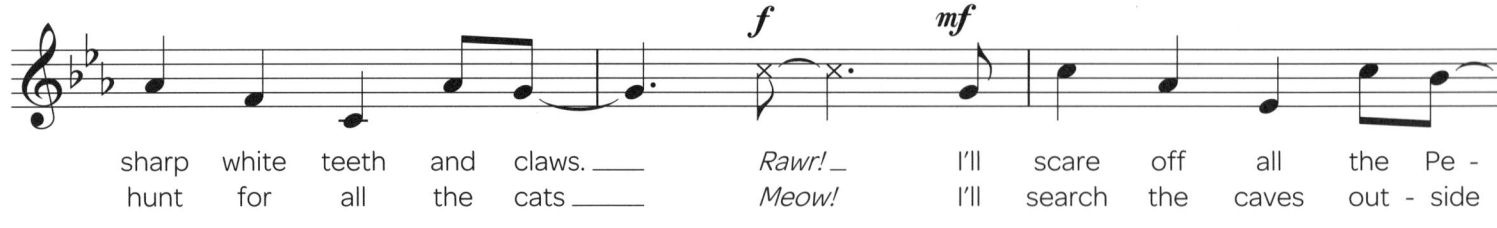

* X noteheads = fun sound effect noise, no specific pitch
** Pekingese: "PEE-kuh-NEEZ" IPA: [ˌpi kə ˈniz]: a breed of small dog (called "toy dogs") with long hair, originally from China. The name means "lion dog," due to the long hair!

Copyright © 2020 by Lisa Neher (ASCAP), DC al Platypus Publishing Company and Kendra Preston Leonard
All Rights Reserved   Used by Permission

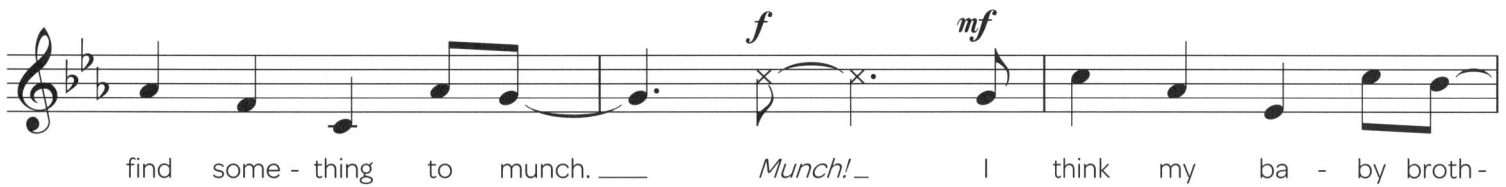

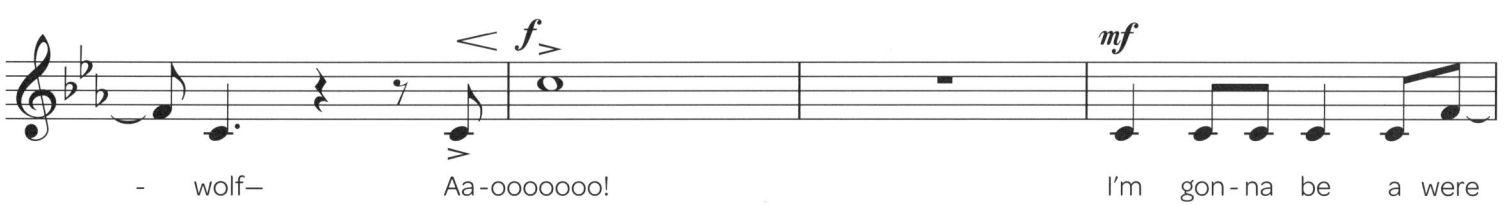
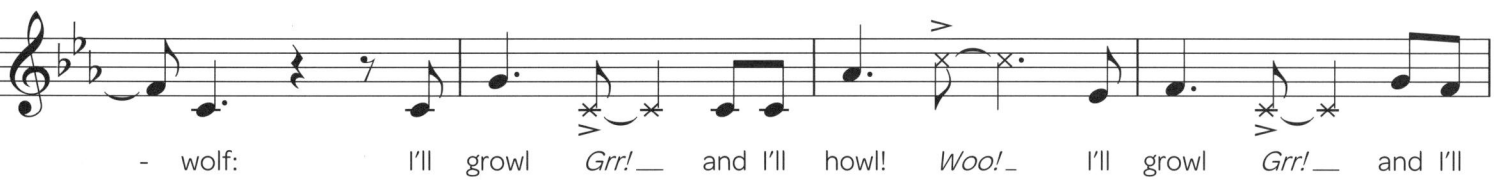
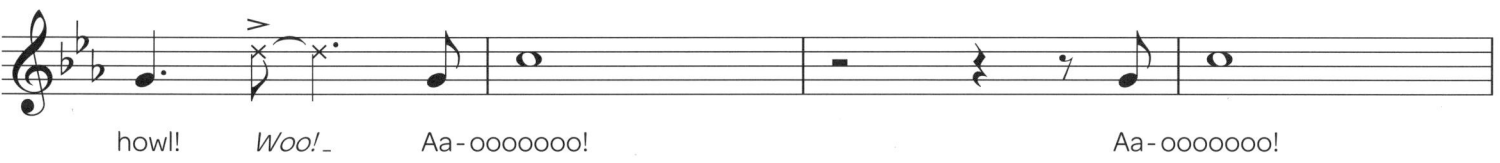
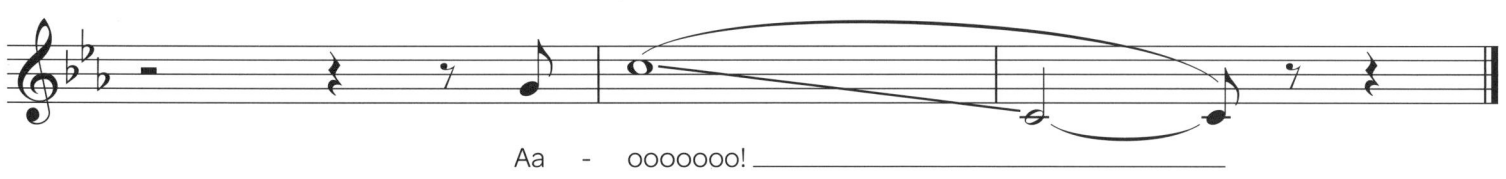

GROWL AND HOWL

Words by Kendra Preston Leonard
Music by Lisa Neher

* X noteheads = fun sound effect noise, no specific pitch

Copyright © 2020 by Lisa Neher (ASCAP), DC al Platypus Publishing Company and Kendra Preston Leonard
All Rights Reserved Used by Permission

* Pekingese: "PEE-kuh-NEEZ" IPA: [ˌpi kə ˈniz]: a breed of small dog (called "toy dogs") with long hair, originally from China. The name means "lion dog," due to the long hair!

49

SONG #9
My Country, 'Tis of Thee

PREPARATION
Stand and listen to this song while marching to the beat.

ACTIVITY
Draw a picture of your nation's flag.

MUSICAL CONCEPT: Style

This song is an American patriotic song. It sounds just like the national anthem of many nations including Great Britain and Northern Ireland: *God Save the Queen/King* (depending on the gender of the current reigning monarch). It uses different text, but the same melody. *Note: This song is not the American national anthem.*

Patriotic songs are well-known melodies and lyrics that celebrate unity and encourage feelings of pride for one's country or nation.

Name another patriotic song you may know: _____

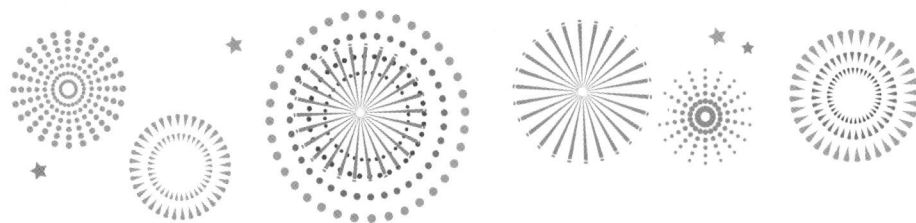

DISCOVERY

This song uses historical language that is older in fashion and style and uses words that seem different from our language today.

The word *Thee* is a fancy and old-fashioned way of saying *You*.

How many times do you sing the word *Thee* in this song? _____

Are there any other unique words in this song you haven't heard before or don't know the meaning of? Practice writing them here and see if you can figure out what they mean.

_____

HOW TO PRACTICE

The words in this song will have more ring in the singing tone if the singer creates tall space for the vowels.

- [ ] Practice speaking the following phrase using tall vowel space: *Mee-Meh-Mah-Moh-Moo*

- [ ] Sing them on a single pitch repeating the same note.

- [ ] Sing them in different parts of your vocal range

Practice first in your lesson with your teacher. Then practice it at home every day.

- [ ] Find various recordings of this song on the internet. Notice how different people perform this famous song.

Which performance is your favorite? _____

PERFORMING: Sing with Confidence and Honor

Think of ways you could sing this song showing pride and honor to your audience as you sing.

- [ ] How do you stand when you want to show pride and honor?

- [ ] Where can you look when you sing about pride and honor? What can you imagine you are looking at?

- [ ] What can you do with your hands when you sing about pride and honor?

MY COUNTRY, 'TIS OF THEE
(America)

Words by Samuel Francis Smith
Music from *Thesaurus Musicus*

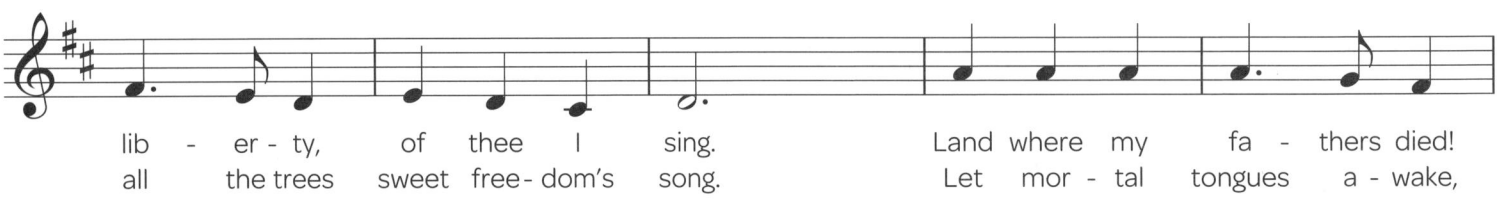

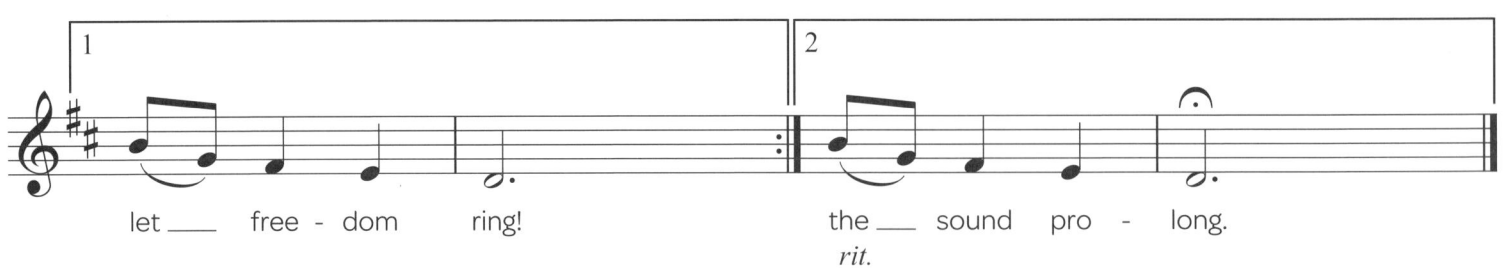

MY COUNTRY, 'TIS OF THEE
(America)

Words by Samuel Francis Smith
Music from *Thesaurus Musicus*

SONG #10
Sleep Gently, Tiny Child

PREPARATION

Listen and move to the beat of this song. Use a scarf or piece of fabric to flow to the beat.

If you were going to sing your lullaby to one of these, who would you like to sing it to?

ACTIVITY

Draw a few vocal exploration lines. Create at least one you think best represents the flow of this melody.

Do you remember what a melody is?

A melody is _____

(see p. 23 for definition as part of the activity for "Umbrellas")

TECHNIQUE: Expression

Read through the text of this song expressing these different emotions:

Angry **Sad** **Happy** **Tired** **Scared** **Goofy**

Which one do you feel is more natural to the mood and beat of the music?

DISCOVERY

Musical Treasure Hunt:

Dynamics in music are symbols used to tell the performer how loud and soft to sing. Here are some common dynamic symbols used in music:

p stands for *piano* in Italian which means soft.

mp stands for *mezzo piano* which means medium soft.

mf stands for *mezzo forte* which means medium loud.

☐ Find the dynamic symbols in your score and circle them.

☐ Hunt in your vocal score and see if you can find notes marked as an X. When you listen to the performance, what do you think that means?

HOW TO PRACTICE

☐ Sing this song while holding your favorite stuffed animal, toy, or doll. Cradle it in your arms tenderly and rock it while you sing. See if you can pretend to put it to sleep.

Which toy did you choose? _____

☐ Sing this song faster and with a louder dynamic (*f* means *forte* which means to sing loud)

Did it have the same effect of gentleness? YES or NO

Why do you think? _____

PERFORMING: Perform Using Dynamics

Perform this song using the dynamics that you circled in your vocal score.

Hint: Sing your dynamics gently and imagine singing your toy to sleep.

SLEEP GENTLY, TINY CHILD

Words and Music by
Donna Rhodenizer

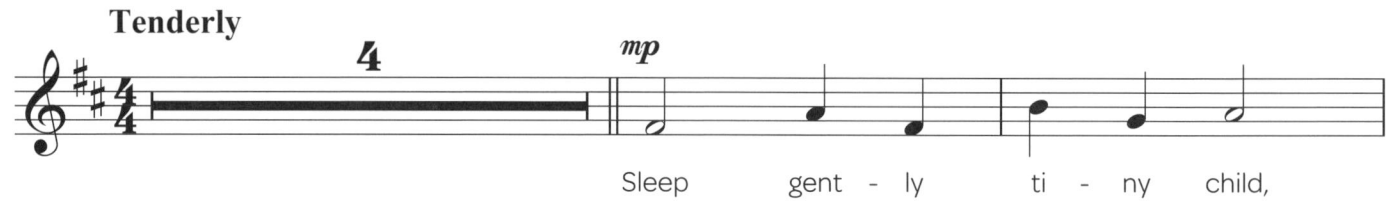
Sleep gent-ly ti-ny child,

Moth-er watch is keep-ing. Rest gent-ly ti-ny babe,

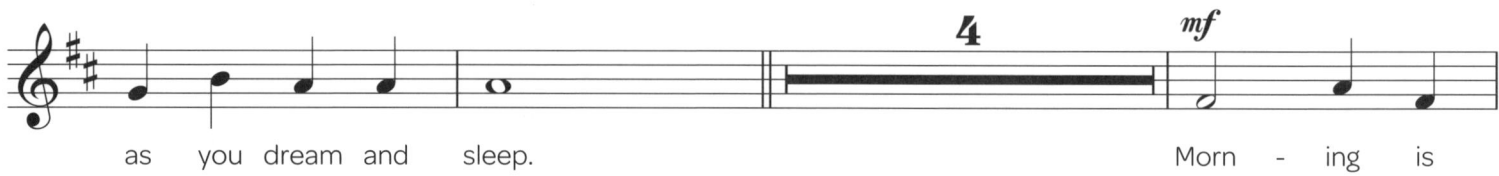
as you dream and sleep. Morn-ing is

com-ing soon, sun-light will come creep-ing. Rest now 'til

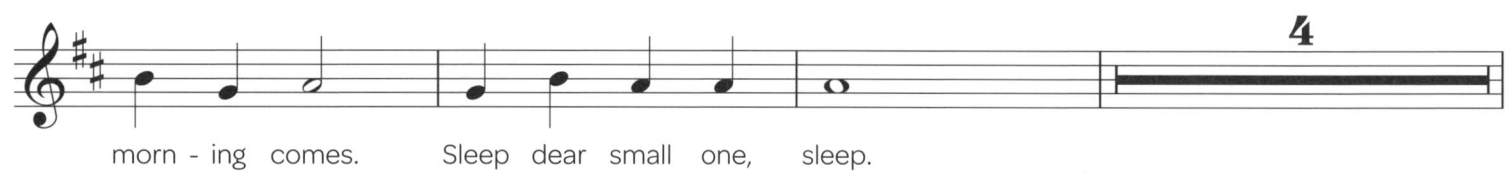
morn-ing comes. Sleep dear small one, sleep.

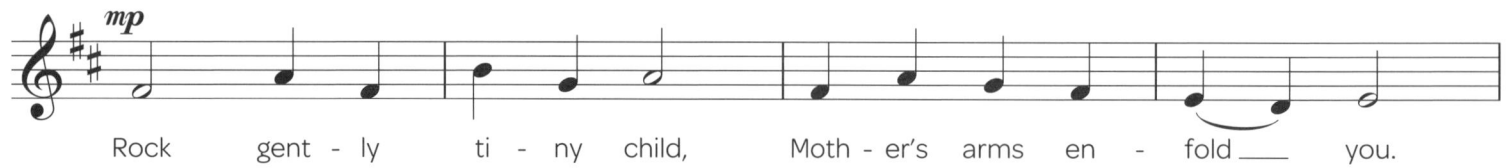
Rock gent-ly ti-ny child, Moth-er's arms en-fold you.

Hush, hear the lul-la-by. Sleep dear ba-by, sleep.

Copyright © 1993 Red Castle Publishing
All Rights Reserved   Used by Permission

SLEEP GENTLY, TINY CHILD

Words and Music by
Donna Rhodenizer

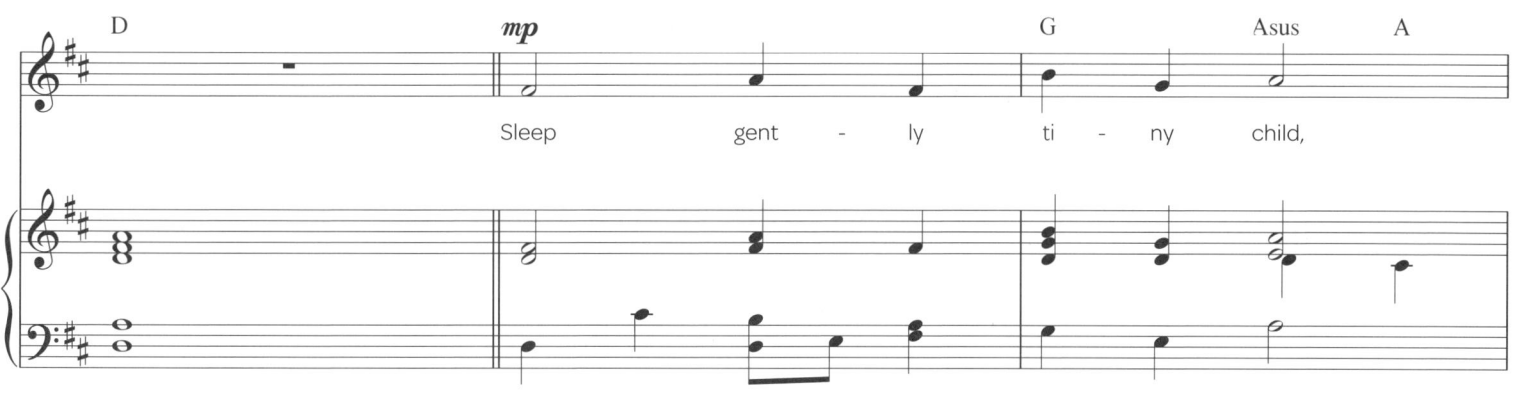
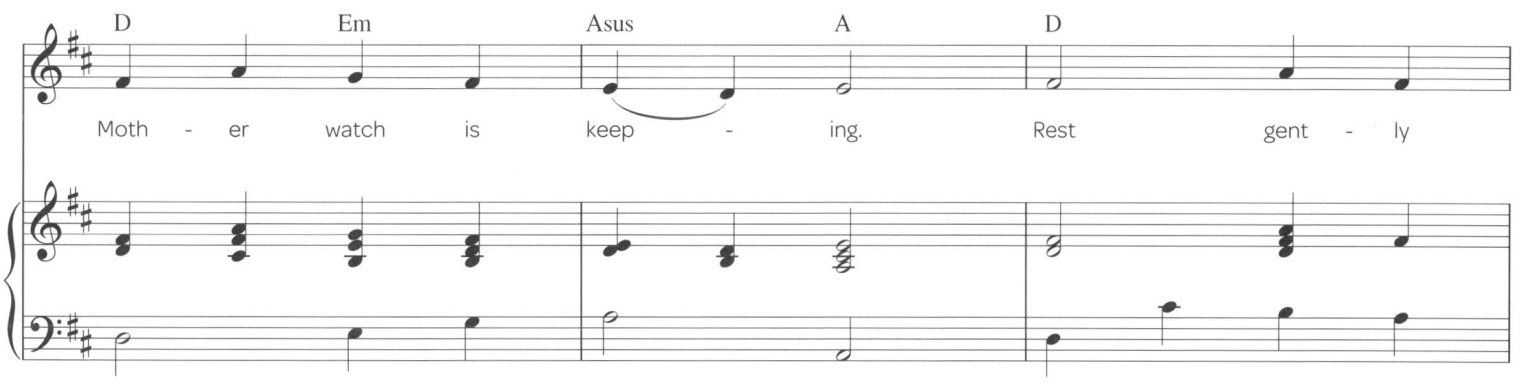

Copyright © 1993 Red Castle Publishing
All Rights Reserved Used by Permission

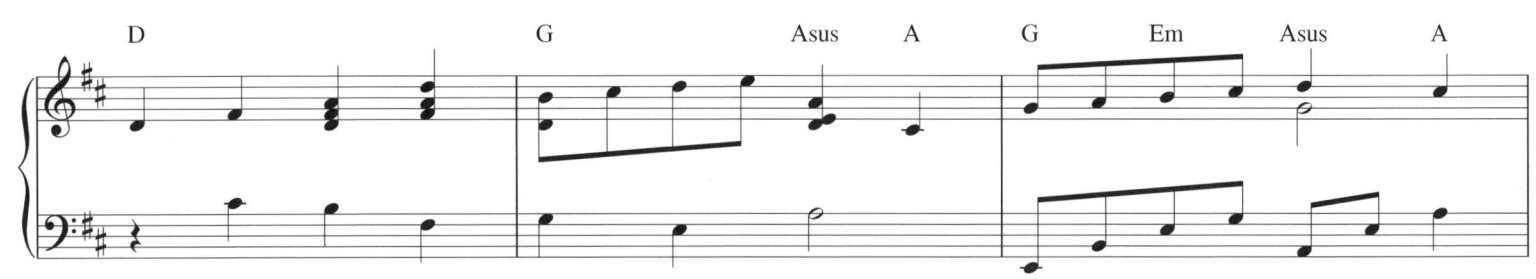
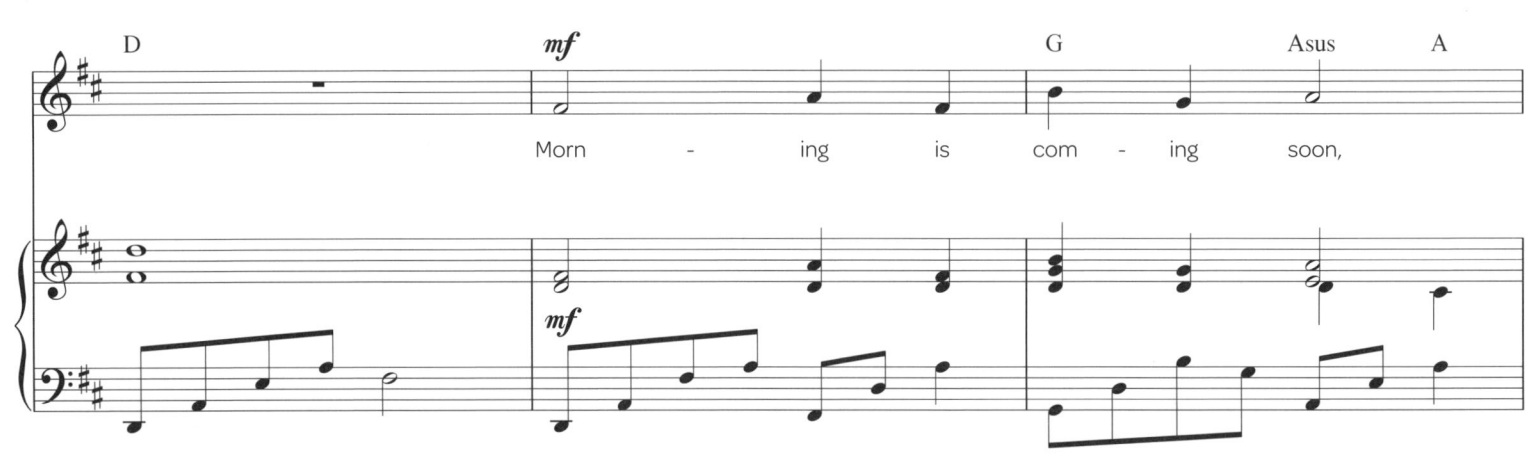
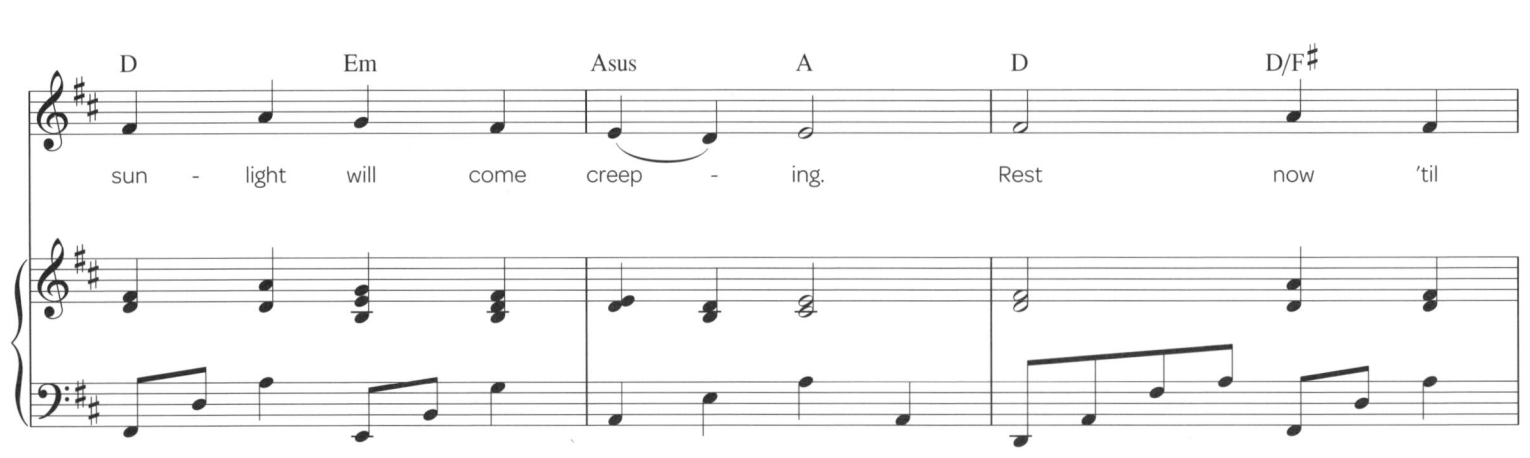
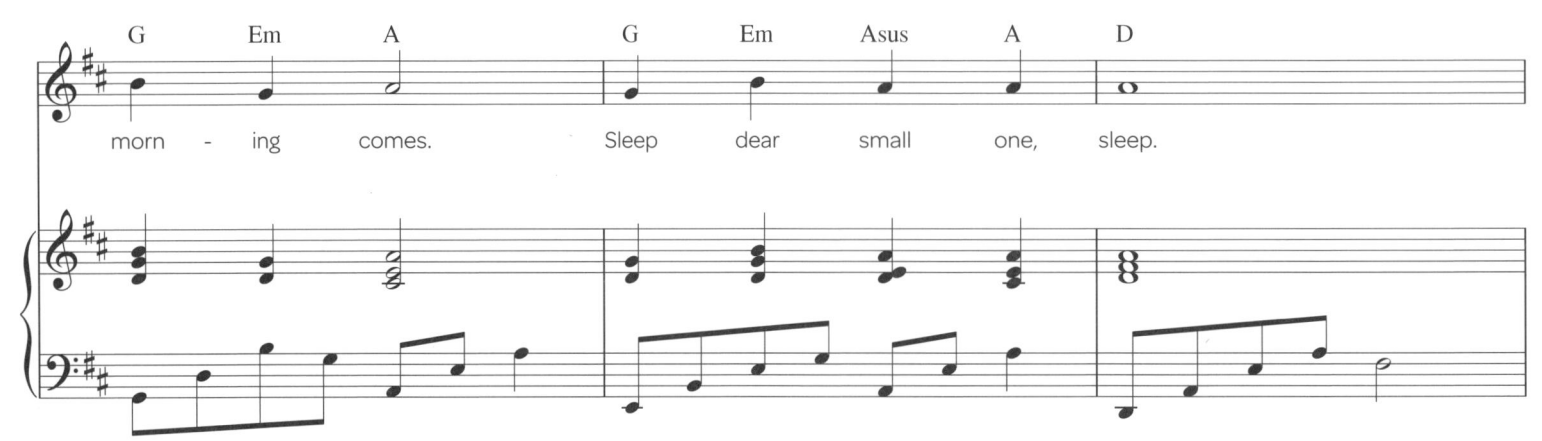

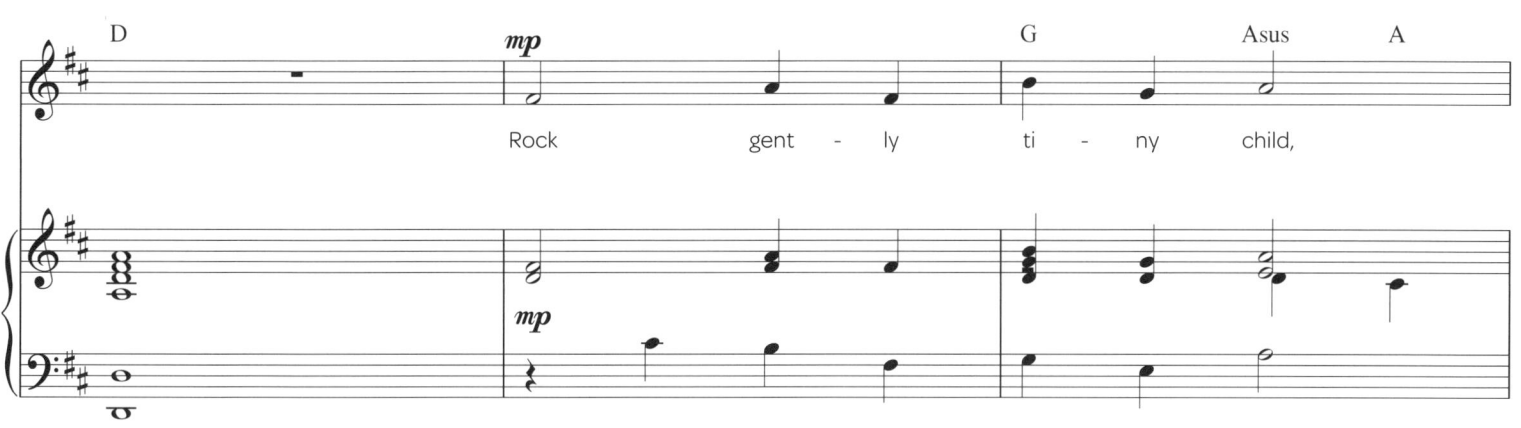
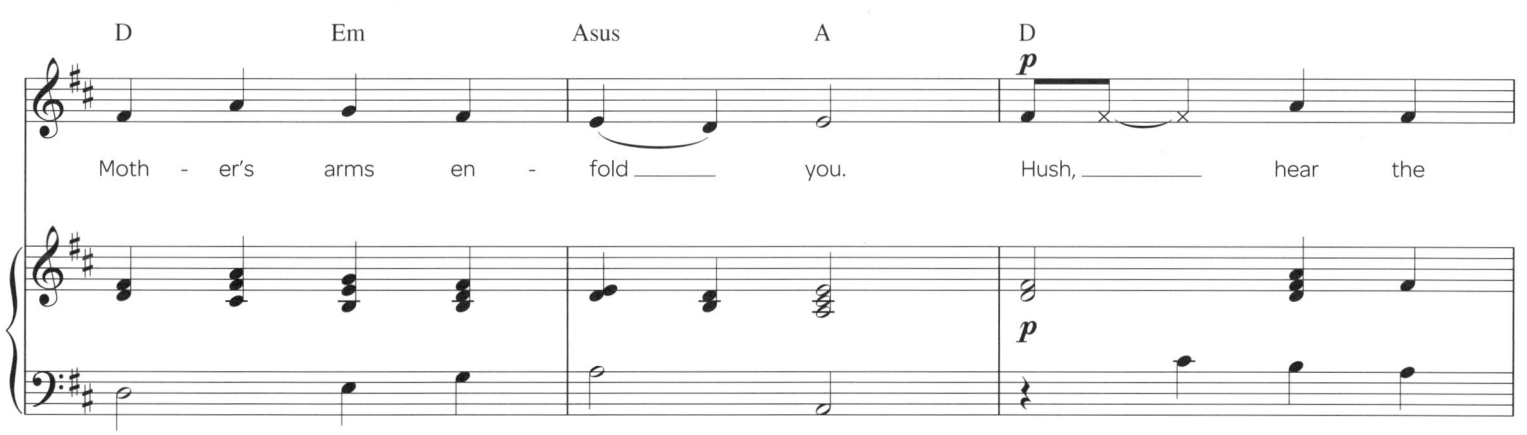

61

SONG #11
Come On Get Happy

PREPARATION

Listen to this song and move to the beat. Notice how differently you move to this beat as compared to the lullaby. Describe the difference to your teacher.

ACTIVITY

What do you love about singing? Do you feel happy when you sing? Draw a picture of things that make you happy.

SINGING TECHNIQUE: Diction

As singers we know how important it is to sing with good diction. But in this song, you might notice some of the words are missing final consonants.

All the words that end in: -ing drop the final letter g. This makes the text more relaxed and informal in this song.

DISCOVERY

This song has a swing beat. A *swing beat* is not as strict as a steady beat and has a more relaxed feel by emphasizing the off-beat.

What other songs have you learned that have a swing beat?

_____

Circle all of the *-ing* word endings that drop the letter *g*. This pronunciation, along with the swing beat, creates a groovy feel.

Even though the text is relaxed, still practice speaking the text to get good diction, but stay groovy and don't pronounce those ending Gs!

HOW TO PRACTICE

☐ Listen to the performance track of this song every day while you are working on it.

☐ Listen to the piano track of this song every day and memorize when to start singing.

☐ Have your teacher help you count in your entrance and practice your counting at home.

PERFORMING: Sing with Groovy Energy

Sing this song with energy and excitement as you communicate to your audience how much you love to sing.

Do you remember to use your slate each time before you perform? If you forgot, review that from page 24.

COME ON GET HAPPY
Theme from *The Partridge Family*

Words and Music by Wes Farrell
and Danny Janssen

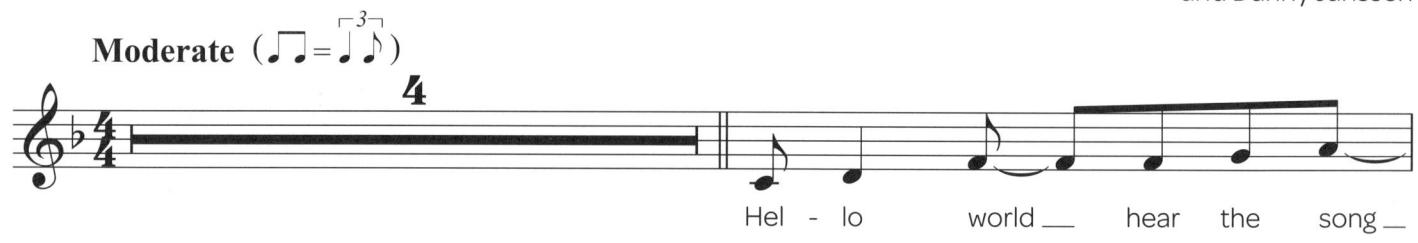

Copyright © 1972 Screen Gems-EMI Music Inc. and Lovolar Music
Copyright Renewed
All Rights on behalf of Screen Gems-EMI Music Inc. in the United States Administered by Sony Music Publishing (US) LLC, 424 Church Street, Suite 1200, Nashville, TN 37219
All Rights on behalf of Lovolar Music in the United States Administered by Bike Music c/o Concord Music Publishing
All Rights for the World excluding the United States Administered by Sony Music Publishing (US) LLC, 424 Church Street, Suite 1200, Nashville, TN 37219
International Copyright Secured   All Rights Reserved

Some-thin' al-ways hap-pens when ev - er we're to-geth-er, we

get a hap-py feel-in' when we're sing-in' a song.

Trav - elin' a - long there's a song that we're sing - in',

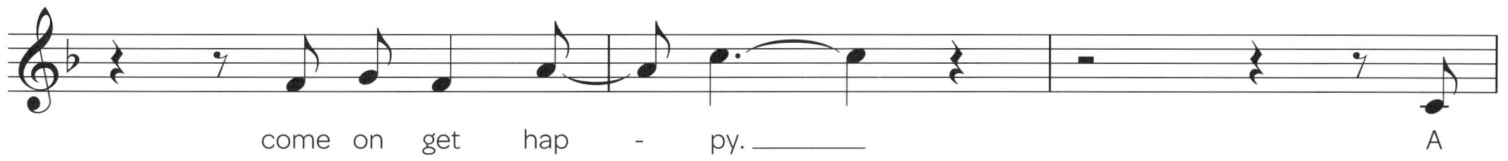
come on get hap - py. A

whole lot of lov - in' is what we'll be bring - in', we'll make you hap-

- py, we'll make you hap - py,

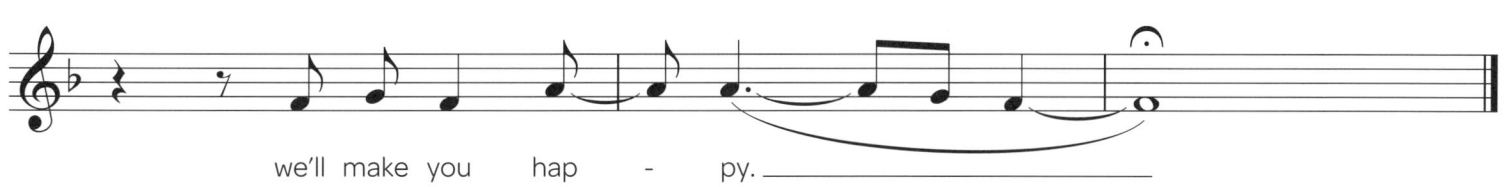
we'll make you hap - py.

COME ON GET HAPPY
Theme from *The Partridge Family*

Words and Music by Wes Farrell
and Danny Janssen

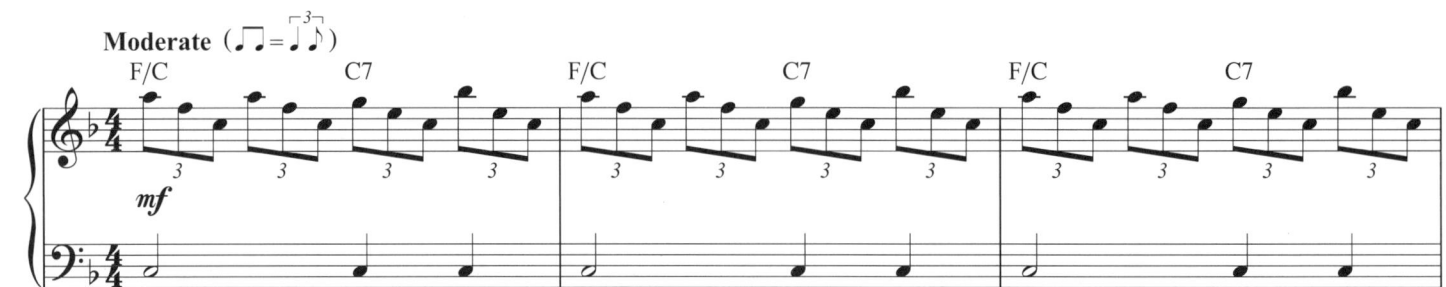

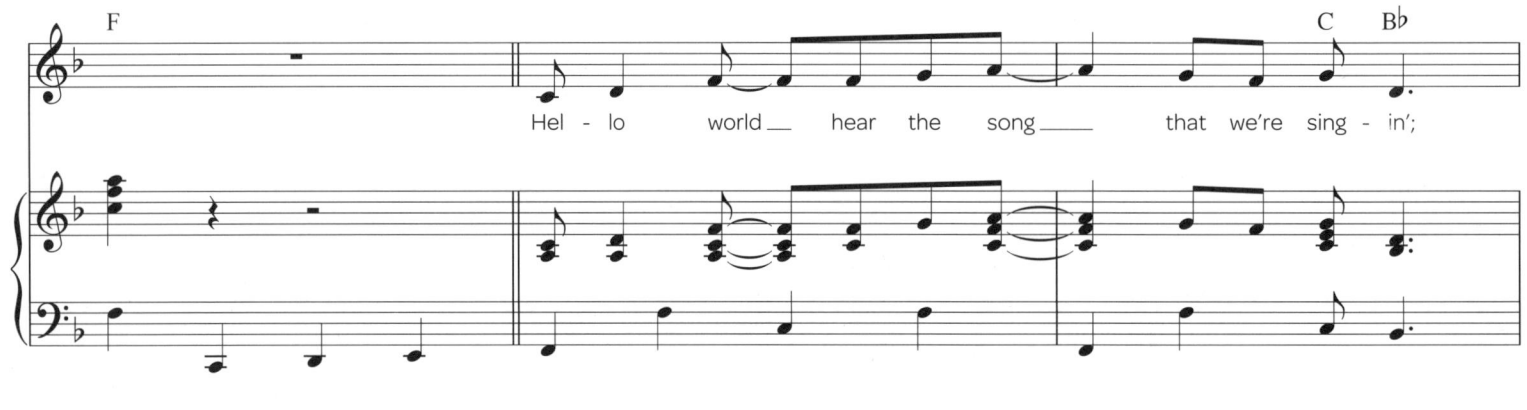

Hel - lo world___ hear the song___ that we're sing - in';

come on get hap - py.___ A

whole lot of lov - in' is what___ we'll be bring - in', we'll make you hap -

Copyright © 1972 Screen Gems-EMI Music Inc. and Lovolar Music
Copyright Renewed
All Rights on behalf of Screen Gems-EMI Music Inc. in the United States Administered by Sony Music Publishing (US) LLC, 424 Church Street, Suite 1200, Nashville, TN 37219
All Rights on behalf of Lovolar Music in the United States Administered by Bike Music c/o Concord Music Publishing
All Rights for the World excluding the United States Administered by Sony Music Publishing (US) LLC, 424 Church Street, Suite 1200, Nashville, TN 37219
International Copyright Secured   All Rights Reserved

SONG #12
Tell Me Your Story

PREPARATION

Listen carefully to the words in this song. What message is the singer communicating to the audience?

_____

_____

How do you move to the beat in this song?
Circle one:

March   **Sway**   **Jump up and down**

Do you move with your whole body or just part of your body?
Do you move quickly or slowly?
Try moving in place and then try traveling across the room while moving to the beat.

ACTIVITY

Echo your teacher in small phrases while you clap a steady beat and chant the words of this song with the correct rhythm.

Review the diction poem on page 33 exercise to warm up your articulation muscles.

SINGING TECHNIQUE: Expression

Why do you think it is important to express the emotion of a song?

_____

As singers, we work to make storytelling and expressive communicating with the audience a very important part of the singing experience. Think about the words you are singing about in this song and explore ways to communicate that to your audience.

DISCOVERY

Who is someone new you have met recently? _____

What did you learn about that person? _____

Where are they from? _____

Have you ever visited the place where they are from? _____

Where were you born? _____

What is your favorite food to eat? _____

Share these with your teacher. They probably didn't know these things about you!

HOW TO PRACTICE

Make up a story about an interesting person you would like to meet. What is their name and where are they from? What makes them unique?

Draw a picture of this person.

Practice singing this song about the person in your picture.

PERFORMING: Sing to Express the Story

How can you express your answers with your audience when you perform? Will you use facial expressions and hand gestures to tell the story?

Be sure to perform this song with good diction so your audience can hear the story you are sharing.

TELL ME YOUR STORY

Words and Music by
Glyn Lehmann

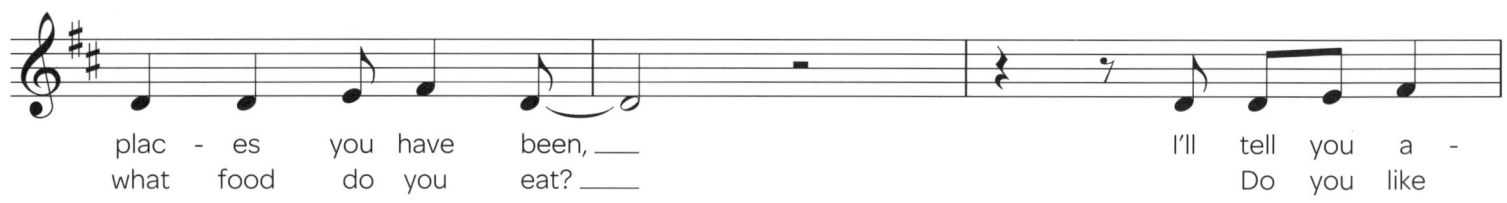
plac - es you have been, _____ I'll tell you a-
what food do you eat? _____ Do you like

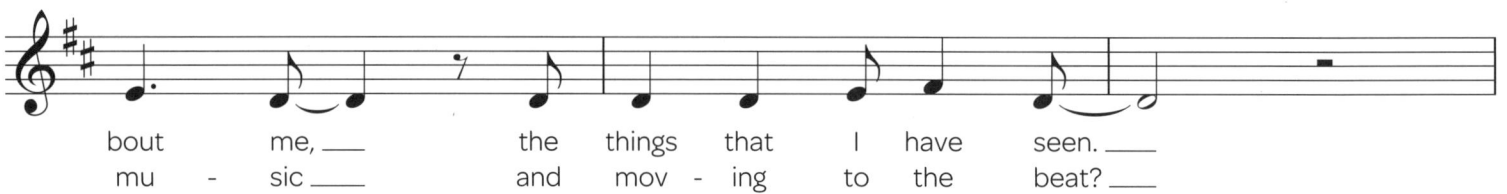
bout me, _____ the things that I have seen. _____
mu - sic _____ and mov - ing to the beat? _____

Where do you come from, _ what is your his - to - ry? _____
I like your name now, _ at first it sound - ed strange. _____

_____ Were you born here _____ or
_____ Now that I know you, _____ I

some where a - cross the sea? _____
would - n't want you to change. _____
We can learn a-

Copyright © 2011 Glyn Lehmann
All Rights Reserved Used by Permission

TELL ME YOUR STORY

Words and Music by
Glyn Lehmann

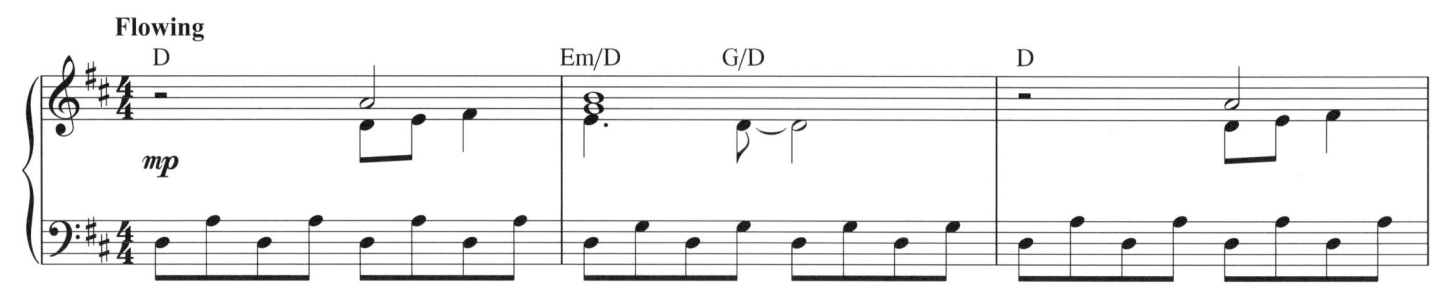

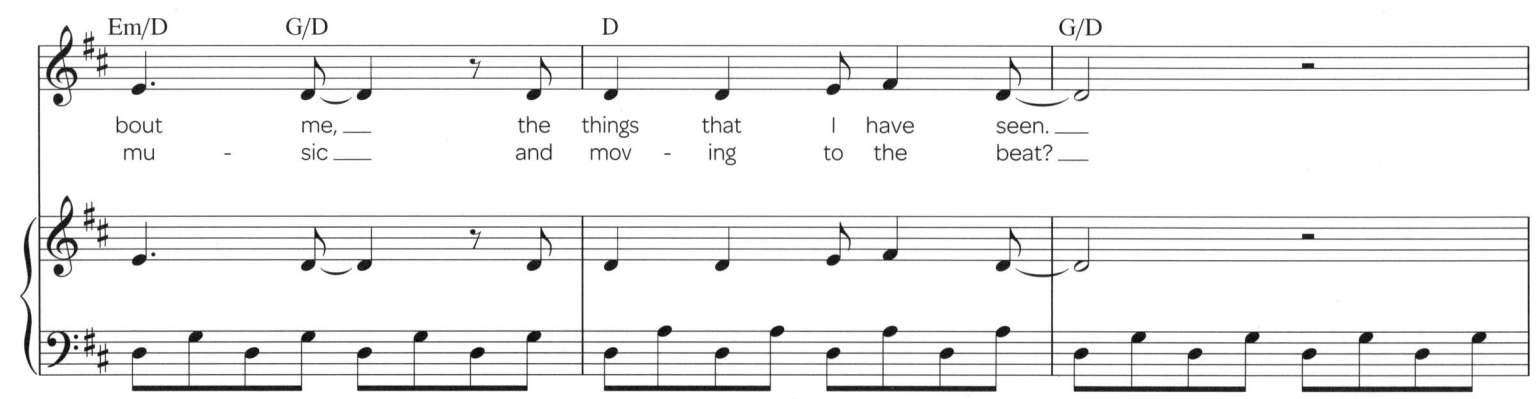

SONG #13
Cleaning!

PREPARATION
Listen to the performance of this song. Observe by using your ears what is happening in the storyline. What do you notice?

ACTIVITY
In music, the person who writes the song is called a composer. The composer in this song offers the singer a chance to change a word in the text. (Find that spot in your vocal score and circle it). Practice using different words and see which one feels natural to you.

Which 2-syllable descriptive word will you use? _____

MUSICAL CONCEPT: Form

This song has different verses. Do you remember what a verse is?
A **verse** is a melodic pattern that can repeat with different text.

How many verses are there in this song? _____

Listen again to this song and circle which expression you hear on each verse.

Verse 1

Verse 2

Verse 3

DISCOVERY

Musical Treasure Hunt:

The composer often gives the performer an idea of how fast or slow the music should go. That is called the tempo marking.

Look in your vocal score and circle the **tempo** marking and the composer's name.

Hint: The composer's name can be found at the top of the score in the upper right-hand corner.

The tempo marking is usually found at the beginning of the song on the left. This tempo marking describes a mood and not a speed. How fast or slow do you think it should be?

Do you like helping around the house when it is time to clean? _____

What is your least favorite cleaning chore? _____

What is one cleaning chore you are good at? _____

HOW TO PRACTICE

Practice expressive singing skills by exploring the different emotions you feel when you are grumpy, happy, and goofy. Sing this song three times with your accompaniment track.
On the line *Oh no!*, try out each of these different expressions:

☐    ☐    ☐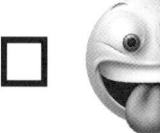

Circle the one that feels natural with the expression and mood of the text you are singing.

PERFORMING: Sing to Convince Your Audience

When you sing this for an audience, make sure your expression reflects your feelings about cleaning!

And remember... If they can understand your words, maybe you can convince someone to never ask you to help with your least favorite chore!

Are you taking a bow after each performance? Always practice taking a bow so it becomes a regular part of your performing skills.

CLEANING!

Words and Music by
Donna Rhodenizer

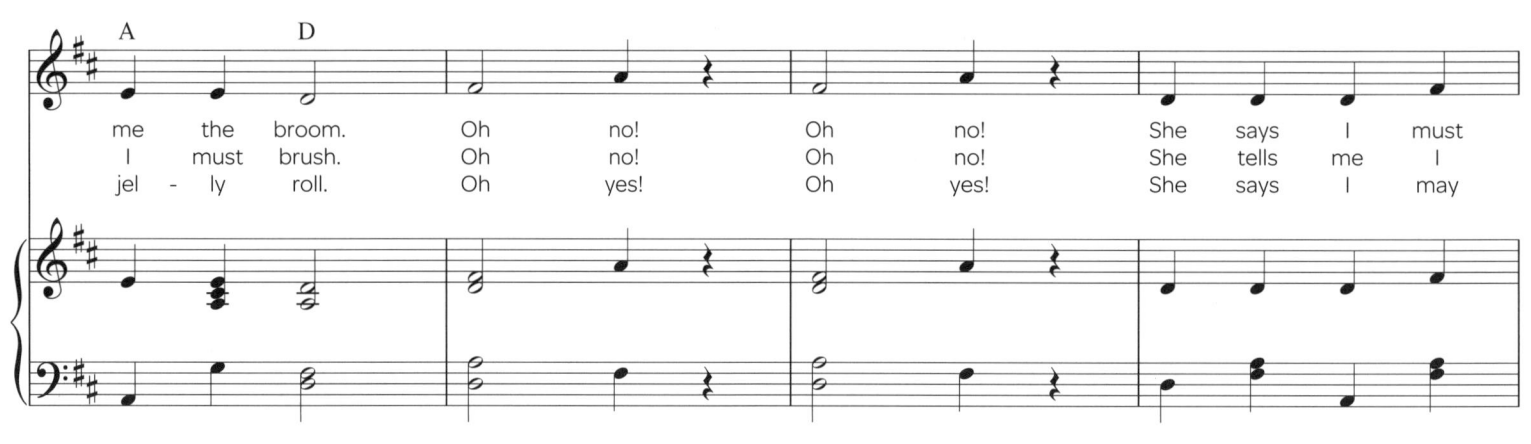

* Singers may choose their own two-syllable adjective!
  ex: vs. 1 - boring, gruesome, awful; vs. 3 - yummy, scrumptious, lovely

SONG #14
Catch a Falling Star

PREPARATION

Listen to the performance of this song. Which of these descriptions best describes the beat of this song?

Steady beat   **Swing beat**   **Combination of swing and steady**

ACTIVITY

This song is about being optimistic. That's when a person is hopeful, positive, and confident about a situation or something to happen.

Draw a picture or describe something you are personally excited and optimistic about that might happen soon in your life.

MUSICAL CONCEPT: Rhythm

Find this rhythm pattern in your vocal score:

Clap this rhythm as a steady beat and as a swing beat.

DISCOVERY

Musical Treasure Hunt:

☐ Locate the word "optimistic" in the vocal score. Highlight or underline this word.

☐ Circle the repeat signs in the vocal score.

☐ Draw both repeat signs here on this music staff:

☐ Repeated melodic notes do not move up or down but stay on the same line or same space. Find notes that repeat on the same line or space and circle them together as a unit.

HOW TO PRACTICE

Review techniques for creating pure vowel sounds.

☐ Practice this exercise thinking about the vowel space to get more ring in your sound:
Mee-Meh-Mah-Moh-Moo

Make sure to sing emphasizing a single vowel sound as you sustain these words on long notes:
Away
Day
Night

☐ Circle these words in your vocal score.

PERFORMING: Sing Feeling Optimistic

Sing this song expressing optimism and share that feeling with your audience.
What kind of facial expression do you make when you feel confident and happy?
What do your hands do when you feel confident and hopeful?
Use those expressions when performing this song.

CATCH A FALLING STAR

Words and Music by Paul Vance
and Lee Pockriss

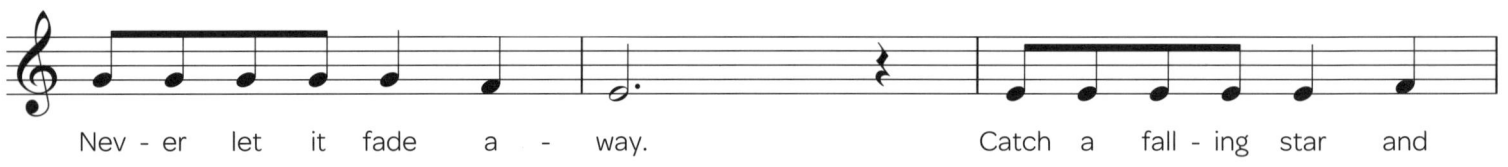

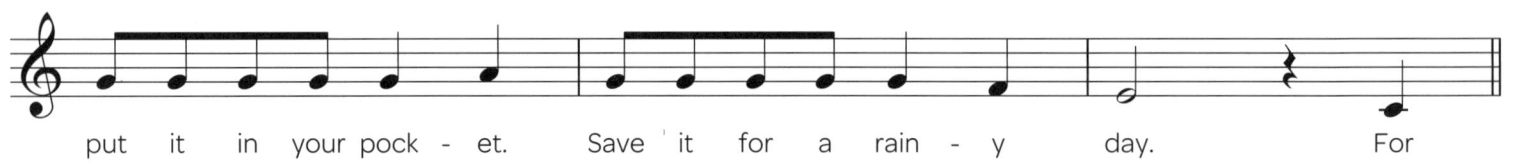

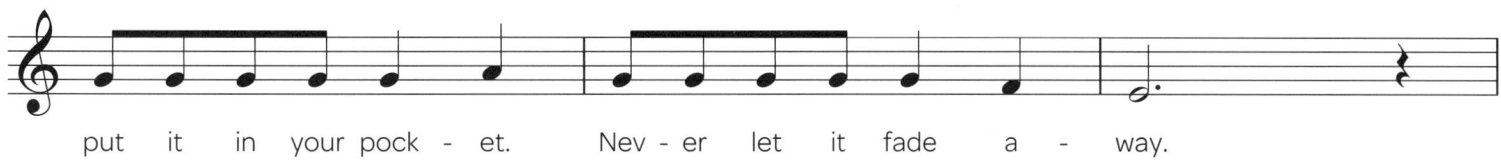

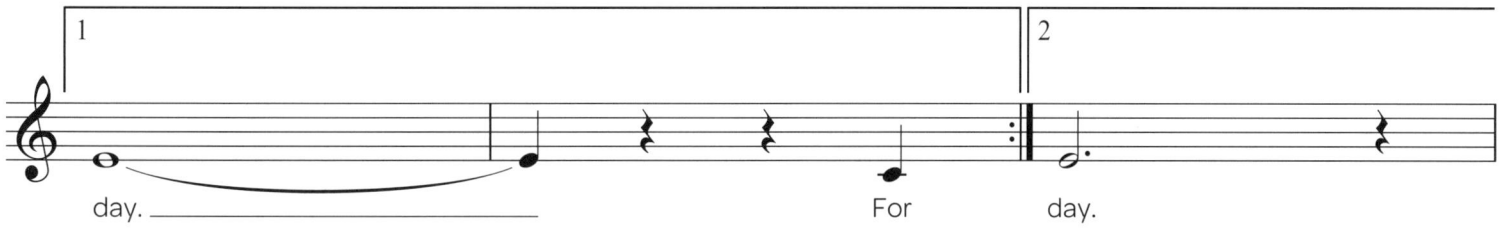

CATCH A FALLING STAR

Words and Music by Paul Vance
and Lee Pockriss

SONG #15
A Step in the Right Direction

PREPARATION

Listen to the performance of this song. There are three different creatures depicted in the story. Write them here:

1. _____   2. _____   3. _____

ACTIVITY

Which creature do you like best? Draw a picture on another piece of paper and share it with your teacher.

SINGING TECHNIQUE: Descending Vocal Exploration

☐ This song starts and ends on the highest note of the melody. Find those two notes (one at beginning and one at end) and circle them.

☐ Follow the descending contour line for a vocal exploration warm-up. Practice descending motion first followed by ascending motion.

☐ Use a light, tall vowel and try it on these sounds to see which one feels most comfortable in your voice: **EE EH AH OH OO**

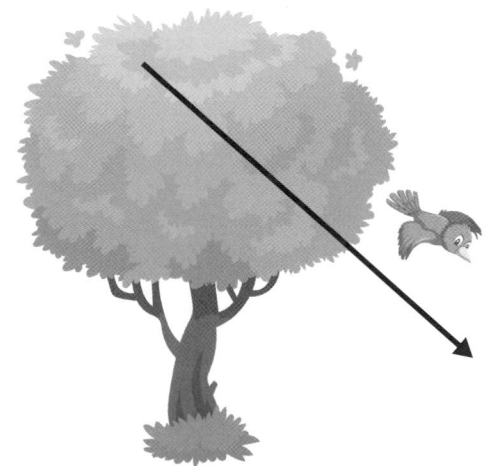
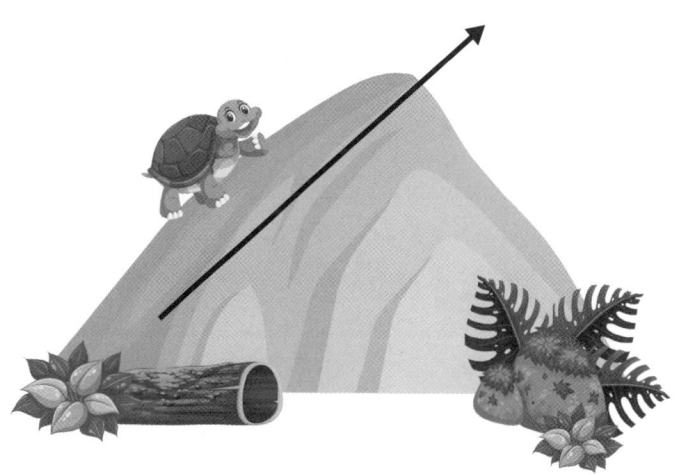

91

DISCOVERY

Musical Treasure Hunt:

Sometimes following along in your vocal score is like reading a map to get directions. Explore your music and find these signs:

☐ Locate the ‖: :‖ and circle them.

There is a new sign to follow in this song. It is like a repeat. When you get to the end of the third ending, the singer is instructed to go back to the 𝄋 and sing until the place that says **To Coda** ⊕, then jump to the final section that says **Coda** ⊕.

☐ Circle or highlight these signs in your vocal score.

Fun fact: Coda means "tail" in Italian. And a song that has a coda ending means it has a little tail at the end!

HOW TO PRACTICE

Speak the text every day. Notice how the words change at the end of each verse to connect to each subject's story.

Tip: Pay attention to the words that rhyme – it will help you remember word order when you memorize.

When you sing about the corresponding subject, which words end that verse?
Draw a line to connect the proper text with the correct subject:

Verse 1   **None the less**

Verse 2   **After all**

Verse 3   **All the same**

PERFORMING: Put All of Your Skills to Work!

Hurray! You made it to the final song in the book. Are you "ready to put your feathers to the test?" Use this checklist to recap all your performing skills when you sing this song for an audience:

- ☐ Sing from memory to focus on your audience while you sing.
- ☐ Use a slate before you perform your song.
- ☐ Think about where to look when you perform your song.
- ☐ Use facial expressions and hand gestures to communicate your story.
- ☐ Take a bow at the end of your performance to say "thank you" for listening.

You did it!! That truly is a step in the right direction!

A STEP IN THE RIGHT DIRECTION
from *Bedknobs and Broomsticks*

Words and Music by Richard M. Sherman
and Robert B. Sherman

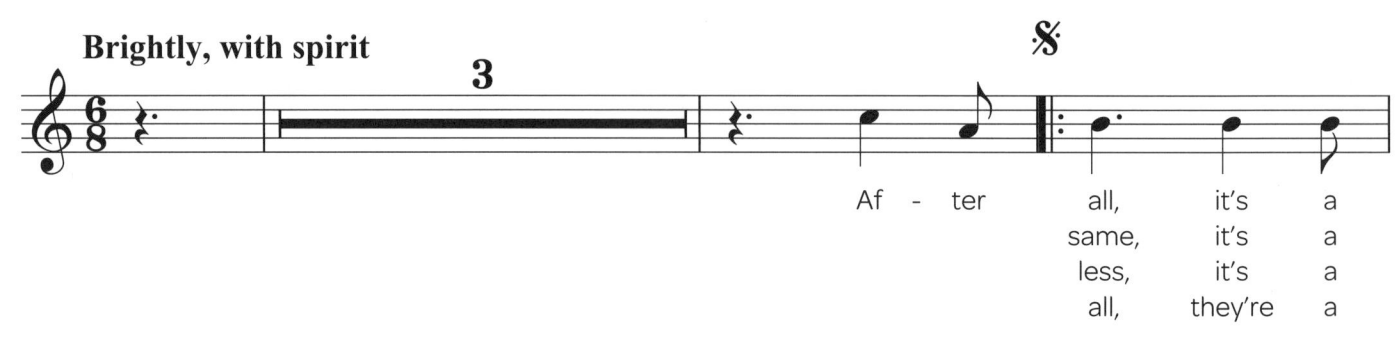

After all, it's a
same, it's a
less, it's a
all, they're a

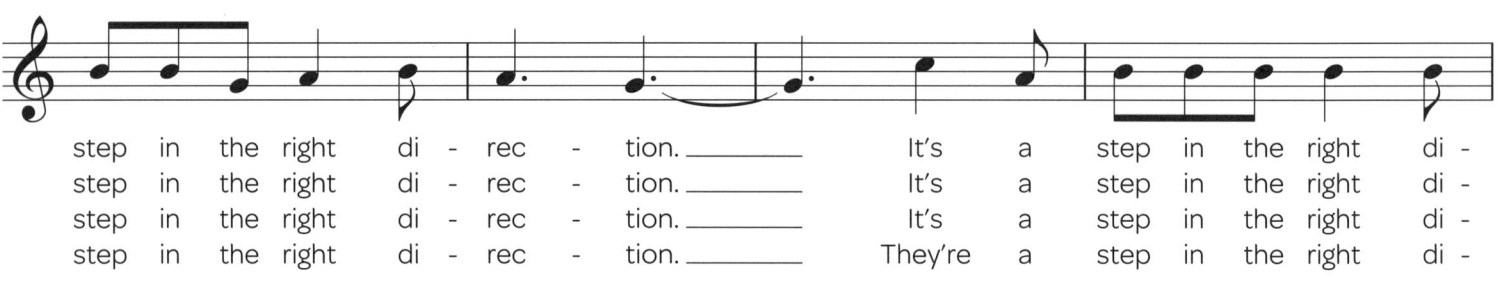

step in the right di - rec - tion. It's a step in the right di-
step in the right di - rec - tion. It's a step in the right di-
step in the right di - rec - tion. It's a step in the right di-
step in the right di - rec - tion. They're a step in the right di-

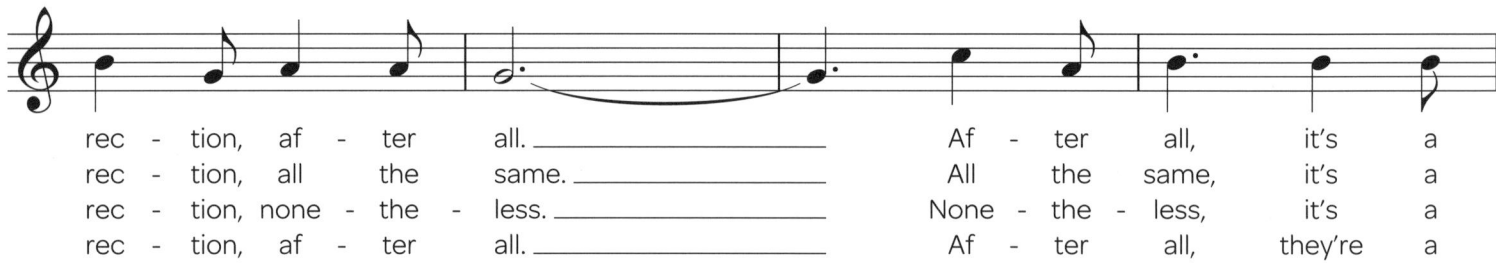

rec - tion, af - ter all. After all, it's a
rec - tion, all the same. All the same, it's a
rec - tion, none - the - less. None - the - less, it's a
rec - tion, af - ter all. After all, they're a

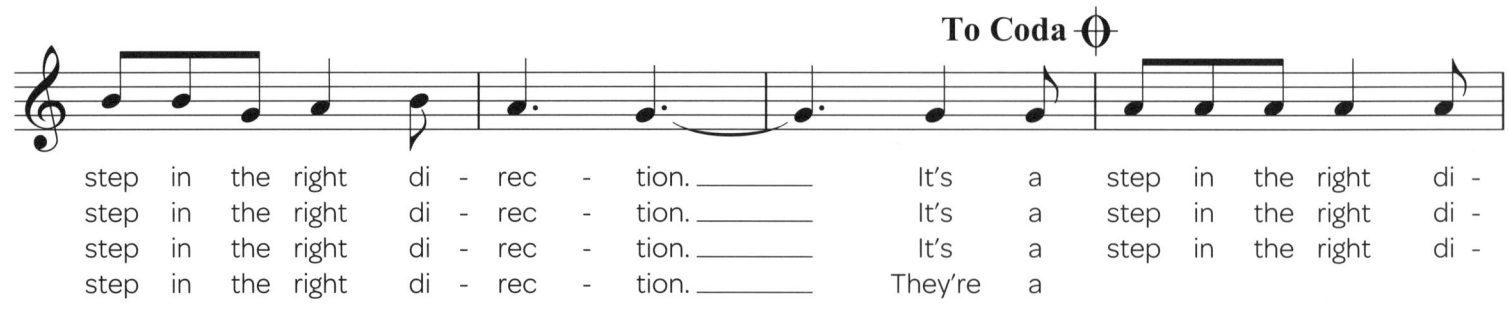

step in the right di - rec - tion. It's a step in the right di-
step in the right di - rec - tion. It's a step in the right di-
step in the right di - rec - tion. It's a step in the right di-
step in the right di - rec - tion. They're a

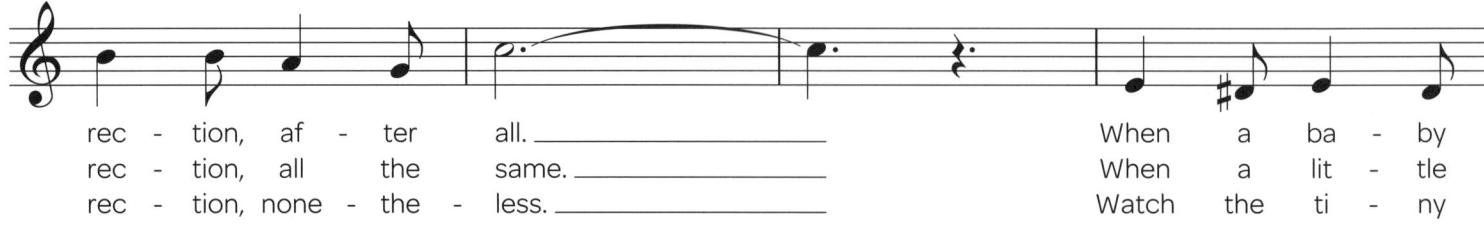

rec - tion, af - ter all. When a ba - by
rec - tion, all the same. When a lit - tle
rec - tion, none - the - less. Watch the ti - ny

© 1969 Wonderland Music Company, Inc.
Copyright Renewed.
All Rights Reserved. Used by Permission.

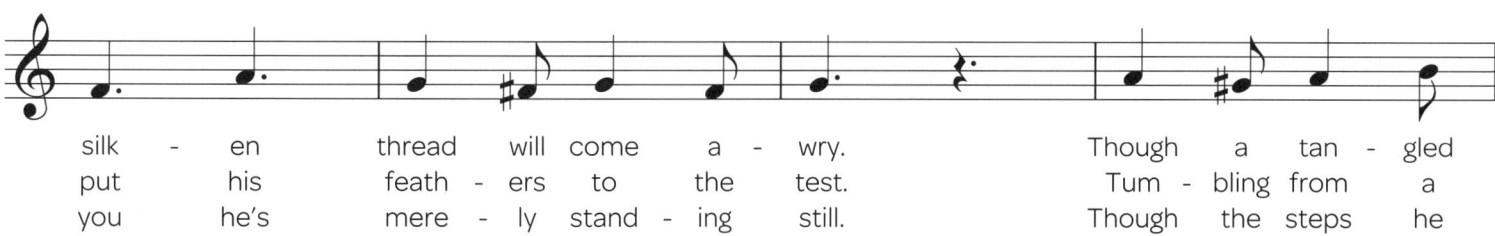

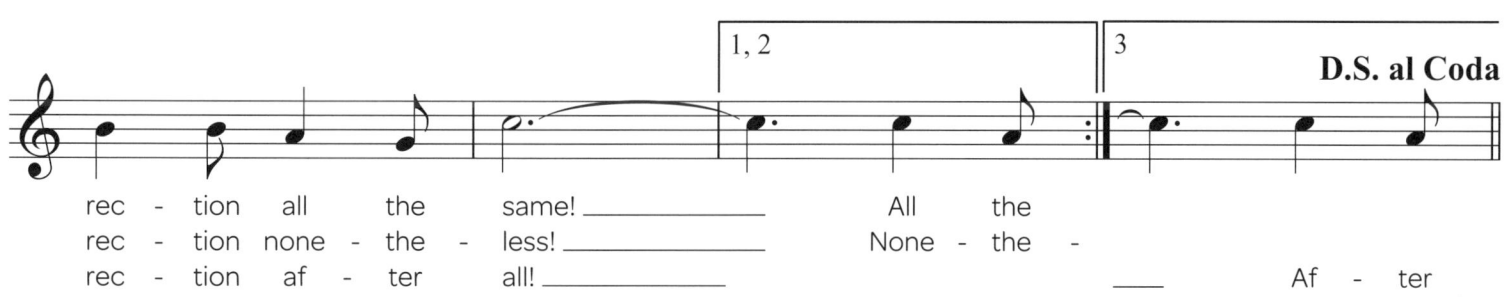

A STEP IN THE RIGHT DIRECTION
from *Bedknobs and Broomsticks*

Words and Music by Richard M. Sherman
and Robert B. Sherman

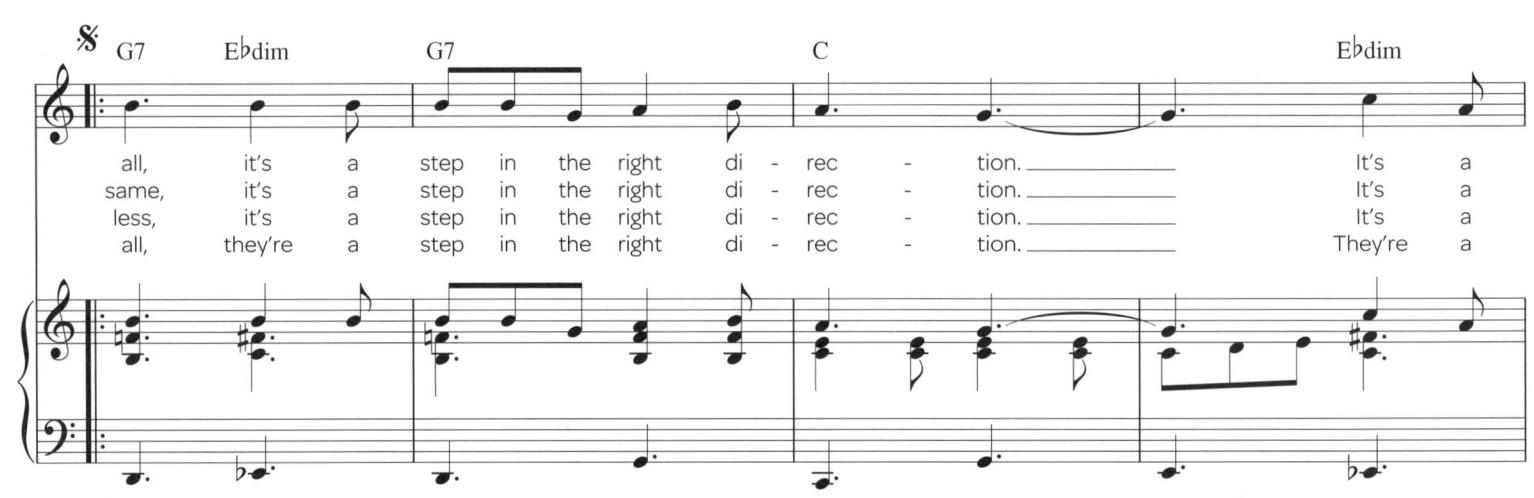

all, it's a step in the right di - rec - tion. ___ It's a
same, it's a step in the right di - rec - tion. ___ It's a
less, it's a step in the right di - rec - tion. ___ It's a
all, they're a step in the right di - rec - tion. ___ They're a

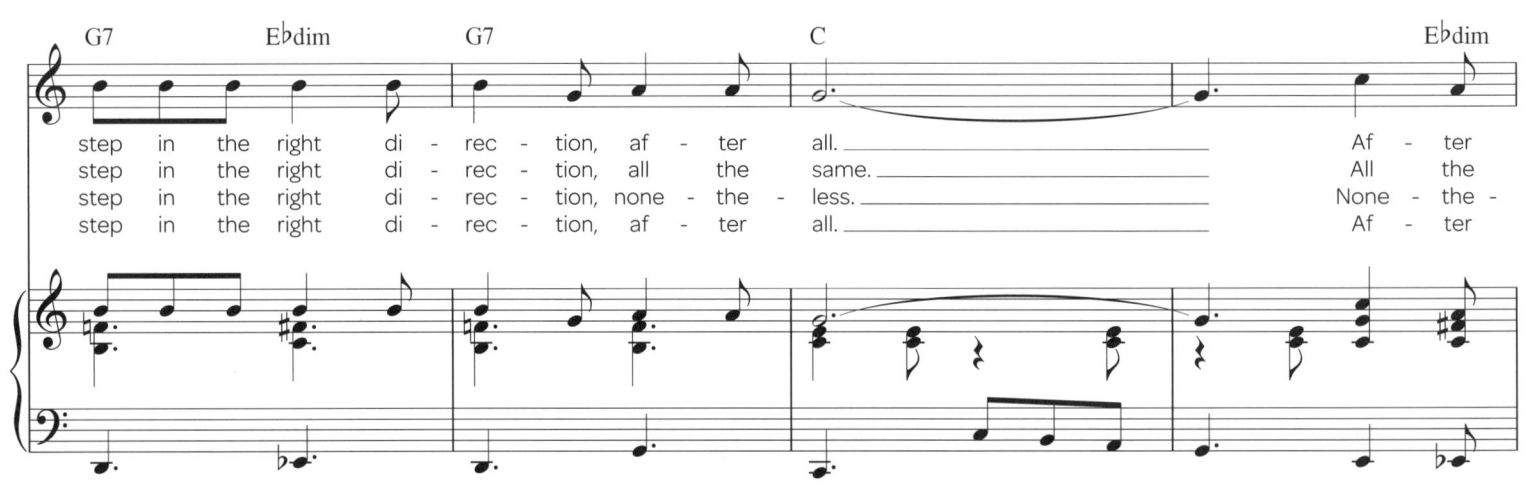

step in the right di - rec - tion, af - ter all. ___ Af - ter
step in the right di - rec - tion, all the same. ___ All the
step in the right di - rec - tion, none - the - less. ___ None - the
step in the right di - rec - tion, af - ter all. ___ Af - ter

© 1969 Wonderland Music Company, Inc.
Copyright Renewed.
All Rights Reserved. Used by Permission.

SINGER'S CHOICE
Title _____

PREPARATION

Listen to your favorite performance of this song. What do you notice about the beat of the song? Is it a steady or swing beat?

ACTIVITY

Draw a picture of what this song makes you think about.

MUSICAL CONCEPT: Dynamics

What are dynamics in music? _____

Dynamics can add more color to the storytelling of a song. What do these dynamics mean?

p: _____

mp: _____

f: _____

mf: _____

Find these symbols in your music score and circle them. If there aren't any, decide where you could sing different dynamics to add expression to your song. Write them in your score.

SINGING TECHNIQUE: Registration

Explore the melody of this song to see if all the notes fit in your vocal range comfortably. Exercise your vocal range by singing vocal exploration lines that explore the high and low range of your selected song.

DISCOVERY

Musical Treasure Hunt:

Study your music score and see if you can find any of these symbols:

𝄞	Treble clef	♩	Quarter note	𝄋	Segno
𝄆 𝄇	Repeat signs	♩	Half note	⊕	Coda

☐ Find the composer's name and circle it. Is there more than one composer name listed?

HOW TO PRACTICE: Make it Your Own

☐ Speak the text every day away from the music

☐ Connect to the text by getting good pronunciation to the words.

☐ Connect to the text by exploring the story and singing it your way.

PERFORMING: Make it Your Own

☐ Sing from memory to focus on your audience while you sing.

☐ Use a slate before you perform your song to get ready.

☐ Think about where to look when you perform your song.

☐ Use facial expressions and/or hand gestures to communicate your story.

☐ Take a bow at the end of your performance to say "thank you" for listening.

Will you use a microphone? If so, make sure to learn how to properly handle the microphone and have fun singing!

Turn to page 107 for your certificate of completion of all these fine songs and singing strategies.

Song Lyrics

I Am a Robot
Words and Music by Kymberly Stewart

I am a robot
I am a robot
I am a robot
And I like to sing
I am a robot
I am a robot
I am a robot
And I like to sing and clap
I am a robot
I am a robot
I am a robot
And I like to sing and clap and dance
I am a robot
I am a robot
I am a robot
And I like to sing and clap
and dance and spin
And I like to sing
I am a robot
I am a robot
I am a robot and my batteries are dead

B-I-N-G-O
Traditional

There was a farmer had a dog and Bingo was his name-o:
B-I-N-G-O,
B-I-N-G-O,
B-I-N-G-O,
And Bingo was his name-o.

There was a farmer had a dog and Bingo was his name-o:
(Clap) I-N-G-O,
(Clap) I-N-G-O,
(Clap) I-N-G-O,
And Bingo was his name-o.

There was a farmer had a dog and Bingo was his name-o:
(Clap) (Clap) N-G-O,
(Clap) (Clap) N-G-O,
(Clap) (Clap) N-G-O,
And Bingo was his name-o.

There was a farmer had a dog and Bingo was his name-o:
(Clap) (Clap) (Clap) G-O,
(Clap) (Clap) (Clap) G-O,
(Clap) (Clap) (Clap) G-O,
And Bingo was his name-o.

There was a farmer had a dog and Bingo was his name-o:
(Clap) (Clap) (Clap) (Clap) O,
(Clap) (Clap) (Clap) (Clap) O,
(Clap) (Clap) (Clap) (Clap) O,
And Bingo was his name-o.

There was a farmer had a dog and Bingo was his name-o:
(Clap) (Clap) (Clap) (Clap) (Clap)
(Clap) (Clap) (Clap) (Clap) (Clap)
(Clap) (Clap) (Clap) (Clap) (Clap)
And Bingo was his name-o.

Twinkle, Twinkle, Little Star
Traditional

Twinkle, twinkle, little star,
How I wonder what you are?
Up above the world so high,
Like a diamond in the sky,
Twinkle, twinkle, little star,
How I wonder what you are?
(2x)

Yes, I really love to sing,
And I love my voice to ring.
I can sing out really strong,
And I love to sing this song,
Yes, I really love to sing,
And I love my voice to ring.

Umbrellas
Words and Music by Donna Rhodenizer

Umbrellas help to keep us dry
When rain is falling from the sky.
Nothing else is quite the same
To keep us dry from falling rain.
Umbrellas help to keep us dry
When rain is falling from the sky.
Sometimes it is hard to wait
Until a rainy day!

I love umbrellas in the spring
When rain falls down on everything.
My umbrella lets me sit and watch
The lovely raindrops drip.
I love umbrellas in the spring
When rain falls down on everything.
Sometimes it is hard to wait
Until a rainy day!

I Like to Sing My ABCs

I like to sing my ABCs
I like singing my ABCs
(2x)

A B C D E F G
H I J K L M N O P
Q R S T U V
W X and-a Y and Z

I sing my ABCs
I like singing my ABCs
I like to sing my ABCs
I like singing my ABCs

A B C D E F G
H I J K L M N O P
Q R S T U V
W X and-a Y and Z
W X and-a Y and Z

Lavender's Blue
Traditional

Lavender's blue, dilly, dilly,
Lavender's green,
When I am king, dilly, dilly,
You shall be queen.

Call up your men, dilly, dilly,
Set them to work,
Some to the plow, dilly, dilly,
Some to the cart.

Some to make hay, dilly, dilly,
Some to cut corn.
While you and I, dilly, dilly,
Keep ourselves warm.

Lavender's green, dilly, dilly,
Lavender's blue,
If you love me, dilly, dilly,
I will love you.

Growl and Howl
Lyrics by Kendra Preston Leonard
Music by Lisa Neher

I'm gonna be a werewolf
Aa-oooooo!
I'm gonna be a werewolf:
I'll growl! Grr!
And I'll howl! Woo!
I'll growl! Grr!
And I'll howl! Woo!
Aa-oooooo!

I'm gonna have a great big tail
And sharp white teeth and claws.
Rawr!
I'll scare off all the Pekingese
And chase the big bulldogs.

I'm a gonna be a werewolf
Aa-oooooo!
I'm gonna be a werewolf:
I'll growl! Grr!
And I'll howl! Woo!
I'll growl! Grr!
And I'll howl! Woo!
Aa-oooooo!

I'll run through all the city streets
And hunt for all the cats
Meow!
I'll search the caves outside of town
And drive out all the bats!

And when I get real hungry,
I'll find something to munch
Munch!
I think my baby brother
Will make a perfect lunch!

I'm a gonna be a werewolf
Aa-oooooo!
I'm gonna be a werewolf:
I'll growl! Grr!
And I'll howl! Woo!
I'll growl! Grr!
And I'll howl! Woo!
Aa-oooooo!

Do-Re-Mi
Lyrics by Oscar Hammerstein II
Music by Richard Rodgers

Doe, a deer, a female deer,
Ray, a drop of golden sun,
Me, a name, I call myself,
Far, a long, long way to run,
Sew, a needle pulling thread,
La, a note to follow sew,
Tea, a drink with jam and bread.
That will bring us back to do, oh, oh, oh

Doe, a deer, a female deer,
Ray, a drop of golden sun,
Me, a name, I call myself,
Far, a long, long way to run,
Sew, a needle pulling thread,
La, a note to follow sew,
Tea, a drink with jam and bread.
That will bring us back to do!

My Country, 'Tis of Thee
Words by Samuel Francis Smith
Music from Thesaurus Musicus

V1
My country, 'tis of thee,
Sweet land of liberty
of thee I sing.
Land where my fathers died!
Land of the Pilgrims' pride!
From every mountainside,
Let freedom ring!

V3
Let music swell the breeze
And ring from all the trees
Sweet freedom's song.
Let mortal tongues awake;
Let all that breathe partake;
Let rocks their silence break,
The sound prolong.

Sleep Gently, Tiny Child
Words and Music by Donna Rhodenizer

Sleep gently tiny child,
Mother watch is keeping.
Rest gently tiny babe,
As you dream and sleep.

Morning is coming soon,
Sunlight will come creeping.
Rest now 'til morning comes.
Sleep dear small one, sleep.

Rock gently tiny child,
Mother's arms enfold you.
Hush, hear the lullaby.
Sleep dear baby, sleep.

Come On Get Happy
Words and Music by Wes Farrell and Danny Jensen

Hello world, hear the song that we're singin';
Come on, get happy.
A whole lotta lovin' is what we'll be bringin',
We'll make you happy.
We had a dream we'd go travelin' together
We'd spread a little lovin', then we'd keep movin' on.
Somethin' always happens whenever we're together,
We get a happy feelin' when we're singin' a song.
Travelin' along, there's a song that we're singin',
Come on, get happy.
A whole lotta lovin' is what we'll be bringin',
We'll make you happy,
We'll make you happy,
We'll make you happy.

Tell Me Your Story
Words and Music by Glyn Lehman

Tell me your story,
The places you have been,
I'll tell you about me,
The things that I have seen.
Where do you come from,
What is your history?
Were you born here
Or somewhere across the sea?

We can learn about each other,
Let's make a start today.
What do we have in common?
We might find we're not so diff'rent anyway!

Tell me your story,
We all have a story to tell.
I'll tell you my story,
Then I'll be a part of yours
And you'll be a part of mine.
We'll write a new story together.

What is your language,
And what food do you eat?
Do you like music
And moving to the beat?
I like your name now,
At first it sounded strange.
Now that I know you,
I wouldn't want you to change.

We can learn about each other,
Let's make a start today.
What do we have in common?
We might find we're not so diff'rent anyway!

Tell me your story,
We all have a story to tell.
I'll tell you my story,
Then I'll be a part of yours
And you'll be a part of mine.
We'll write a new story together.

Cleaning!
Words and Music by Donna Rhodenizer

Mom just handed me the broom.
Oh no! Oh no!
She says I must clean my room.
Oh no!
If I do it very, very fast,
Very, very, very very fast;
Maybe I can quickly do this dreadful task!
Mom just handed me the broom.
Oh no! Oh no!
She says I must clean my room.
Oh no!

Mom just told me I must brush.
Oh no! Oh no!
She tells me I must not fuss.
Oh no!
Teeth need lots of brushing,
There must be no rushing;
Flossing each and every tooth before I'm done!
Mom just told me I must brush.
Oh no! Oh no!
She tells me I must not fuss.
Oh no!

Mom just made a jelly roll.
Oh yes! Oh yes!
She says I may lick the bowl.
Oh yes!
If I eat it slow not fast,
I can make the moment last;
Cleaning up the batter is an awesome task!
Mom just made a jelly roll.
Oh yes! Oh yes!
She says I may lick the bowl.
Oh yes!

Catch a Falling Star
Words and Music by Paul Vance and Lee Pockriss

Catch a falling star and put it in your pocket.
Never let it fade away.
Catch a falling star and put it in your pocket.
Save it for a rainy day.

For love may come and tap you on the shoulder
Some starless night.
Just in case you feel you want to hold her,
You'll have a pocketful of starlight.

Catch a falling star and put it in your pocket.
Never let it fade away.
Catch a falling star and put it in your pocket.
Save it for a rainy day.

For when your troubles start in multiplying
And they just might,
It's easy to forget them without trying,
With just a pocketful of starlight.

Catch a falling star and put it in your pocket.
Never let it fade away.
Catch a falling star and put it in your pocket.
Save it for a rainy day.
Save it for a rainy day.

A Step in the Right Direction
Words and Music by Richard B. Sherman and Robert B. Sherman

After all, it's a step in the right direction
It's a step in the right direction after all
After all, it's a step in the direction
It's a step the right direction after all

When a baby spider tries to trap a fly
Often times, the silken thread will come awry
Though a tangled web is all that he can claim
It's a step in the right direction all the same

All the same, it's a step in the right direction
It's a step in the right direction all the same
All the same, it's a step in the right direction
It's a step in the right direction all the same

When a little sparrow wants to leave the nest
First he has to put his feathers to the test
Tumbling from a treetop can't be called success
But, it's a step in the right direction nonetheless

Nonetheless, it's a step in the right direction
It's a step in the right direction nonetheless
Nonetheless, it's a step in the right direction
It's a step in the right direction nonetheless

Watch the tiny totters inching up a hill
It may seem to you he's merely standing still
Though the steps he takes are infinitely small
They're a step in the right direction after all

After all, it's a step in the right direction
It's a step in the right direction after all
After all, it's a step in the right direction
It's a step the right direction after all

CONGRATULATIONS!

THIS CERTIFICATE IS PRESENTED TO

_____

FOR COMPLETING

Singing Kids' Songbook

_____
Teacher's Signature

_____
Date